Outside

ADVENTURE TRAVEL

MOUNTAIN BIKING

ROB STORY

Outside
BOOKS

W. W. NORTON & COMPANY
NEW YORK • LONDON

For information about permission to reproduce selections from this book, write to
Permissions, W. W. Norton & Company, Inc.
500 Fifth Avenue, New York, NY 10110

The text of this book is composed in Perpetua
with the display set in Monkey
Project Management by Julie Stillman
Composition by Sylvie Vidrine
Manufacturing by Dai Nippon Printing Company
Map Illustrations by Janet Fredericks

Book design by Bill Harvey

Library of Congress Cataloging-in-Publication Data

Story, Rob.
    Mountain biking / Rob Story.
            p. cm. -- (Outside adventure travel)
    "Outside Books."
    Includes bibliographical references (p.) and index.
    1. all terrain cycling. I. Title. II. Series

GV1056 .S76 2001
796.6'3--dc21
                                                    00-048119
            ISBN 0-393-32071-5 (pbk.)

W. W. Norton & Company, Inc., 500 Fifth Avenue, New York, N.Y. 10110
            www.wwnorton.com
W. W. Norton & Company Ltd., 10 Coptic Street, London WC1A 1PU

            1 2 3 4 5 6 7 8 9 0

To M'Lissa,
My Lycra-clad muse

ACKNOWLEDGMENTS

This book wouldn't be possible without the help and influence of many others. I'd like to send thanks to:

My parents, Pete and Harriett, for always encouraging me to write. To my brother and sister, for awakening me to the wonders of Rob-powered locomotion, even if I didn't always enjoy being ridden down our carpeted staircase in suburban Kansas City.

To Aaron Teasdale and David Story for their invaluable help with the Bolivia and Hood River chapters, respectively. To Marshall Sella, for reading copy when it's still as raw and messy as a furball. To Michael Di Gregorio, for tirelessly lending an ear and inspiration.

To Eric Hagerman, Laura Hohnhold, Hal Espen, Leslie Weeden, and all the editors at *Outside* magazine for helping put this book together and for tolerating my ensuing blown deadlines. To the crew who worked with me at *Bike* magazine—especially Mike Ferrentino, Michael Foley, Michael Welman, Steve Casimiro, David Reddick, Keith Carlsen, Rob Reed, Liz Buckingham, Brent Diamond, Ben Warner, and Vernon Felton—for creating and refining the art of mountain bike travel journalism. To all the photographers who've put up with me on assignments.

To Johnny Dodd, James Harvey, Greg Hayward, Brian O'Neill, Joe Sagona, and Rich White, for rarely refusing a ride. To assorted Shawnee Mission East High School Lancers, for somehow helping me live this long.

To Bezo, whose four furry legs run a little happier on singletrack. And finally, to my wife M'Lissa, both for helping guide me into the wonderful world of mountain biking and for tolerating all kinds of research and writing absences since.

CONTENTS

INTRODUCTION

If you're reading this book, chances are you like to explore new places on your mountain bike. You share your lifetime's great rides with your friends, and hope they do the same. You might identify with a mountain biking trip I enjoyed a while back, taking my wife M'Lissa and two friends (David and Joe)—all of them native Californians—on a mountain bike excursion to Missouri, the state where I was born.

In the process of riding singletracks all over Missouri's Ozark Mountains, my West Coast comrades became fascinated with limestone caverns and hay bales. They encountered all manner of new things. On one warm June evening we rode a park near Springfield. As the sun began slipping behind Kansas, we hung a sharp left onto a trail called Flyblow Hollow. The path entered a darkening, primordial forest. A creek tinkled down the hollow. Ferns and trees bent over the trail as if to touch it. Soon, fireflies appeared, pinpoints of light blinking gently up and down the green tunnel. David, like most Californians, had never seen a firefly. He seemed moved by the sight of the tiny floating beacons, kindly illuminating our sylvan path with their momentary incandescence. Since I was moved, too, I declined to tell him that kids back home used to whack fireflies with tennis rackets.

The four of us kept spinning into the inky night—riding without mechanical problems, in ideal temperatures, on a smooth path that seemed purpose-built for two wheels connected by metal tubes. We pedaled and coasted in a captivated silence, catching peripheral glances of each other's soft silhouettes floating through the woods. When we finally returned to the trailhead and our van at 10 o'clock, our punch-drunk high-fives seemed a pitifully inadequate way to celebrate the ride. Then again, they always are.

Like many of you, this book maintains that cycling is the single best way to travel. A bike provides us an unrivaled ability to see the true nature of a foreign place. Mountain bikers aren't like those travelers who fly a thousand miles to a place and never touch its ground. For example, out-of-towners consider lower New York and upper New Jersey an indistinguishable swath of Eastern Seaboard. But ride each place—the exposed roots and glacially deposited rocks of New York's Catskills; the sandy, loamy Pine Barrens of New Jersey—and you'll find two utterly different landscapes located no more than a hundred miles from each other.

Another example: I biked around Newfoundland with some other friends a few years ago. On our first ride, we pedaled a gravel road

Opposite: Refreshing stream crossing, Pocahontas County, West Virginia. Above: Blue streak, Big Bear Lake, California.

through a quiet neighborhood to the trailhead. As we spun slowly along, we could hear the homeowners chatting over their fences, smell what they were cooking for dinner, and see that they largely favored curtains of white lace. In that moment, we learned more about the real Newfoundland than all the tourist brochures of whales and icebergs and fishing boats could ever teach.

On your bike, the land unrolls beneath you at a perfect pace, one tire revolution at a time. Automobiles move too fast to really see the country. Walking moves too slowly to cover sufficient ground. But bikes are like the microfilm machines in the library, where you can go ploddingly slow or dizzyingly fast and see everything you need to see. (Unlike whirring microfilm machines, of course, bikes never induce a sudden onslaught of motion sickness that nearly causes you to hurl all over the card catalog monitors.)

When forced to travel somewhere without my bike, I sometimes feel as silly as the scene in *National Lampoon's Vacation* when Chevy Chase as Clark Griswold nods at the magnificence of the Grand Canyon for five seconds, then turns around and splits. While the Clark Griswolds on their Grayline buses are *viewing* their tourist attractions, we mountain bikers can be out *experiencing* them.

Take this friend of mine who moves all about the country with his bike. When he gets to a fork in the trail, he goes left. He figures if he keeps coming to forks and keeps turning left, eventually he'll wind up where he started. In the meantime, he sees what there is to see and soaks up the essence of the place.

While road-riding packages are well established in the travel industry, mountain bike tourism is a relatively new phenomenon. Some riders approach it like a ski trip: They make hotel reservations, stay in one community, and hire both guides and equipment. Other riders travel like transient rock climbers: They drive a VW bus from trailhead to trailhead, ride singletracks on their own bikes, navigate via their own maps or guidebooks, camp out afterward, and spend money only on food and beer. So long as one enjoys the ride, either mode works just fine.

It's not necessarily easy to mountain bike far from home. Airlines levy absurd surcharges on passengers who bring their bikes. The bulk of bikes and their cases can make travel a pain. After all, nobody wants to lug his bags and a 5-x-3-foot box onto a subway or shuttle bus.

The question is, is it worth the hassle to be able to ride foreign places on your own, familiar bike? Many travelers would say yes. Rental bikes

Above: Campsite with a view, Canyonlands National Park, near Moab, Utah.
Opposite: Mountain biker Richie Schley at Champéry, Switzerland.

are often a gamble, especially overseas, where modern technology has not yet arrived and where bike maintenance is hardly a priority. Some outfitters don't know the difference between a "mountain bike" and a rusted, 40-pound beach cruiser—and they wouldn't tell you if they did. Rental bikes are more reliable in North America, but the quality of rental fleets varies widely.

On the other hand, if you plan to travel for months and only mountain bike sporadically, you'll likely want to rent bikes. If so, do your homework. Ask outfitters what kind of bikes they rent. Ensure that they'll rent you the model you want in the size you want on the day you want. Make deposits if you have to.

Should you ride with mountain bike tour guides? Well, local knowledge always helps. And a guide that both looks after your safety and shows you the area's best trails can save a

lot of headaches. But again, do your homework. Determine what the guide gives you for the money. Don't pay $400 a day to be led on easily found rides in public parks and be fed peanut butter and jelly sandwiches.

What makes a great ride? It depends on the beholder. The mountain biking beholder at whom this book is aimed believes that (1) dirt roads are fun to ride when the scenery appeals and the slope is challenging, and (2) singletrack is almost always better. This belief explains the book's eight chapters on the continental United States alone. It just so happens that the nation that invented mountain biking builds and maintains the best recreational singletracks. Everything about the United States—our weather, our geology, our geographic size, and our late-developing history in the New World—has favorably affected our country's networks of trails. Between the Bureau

of Land Management, the U.S. Forest Service, and state and regional parks, there are vast acres of public lands. Americans' great gobs of disposable income means people can afford bikes and can afford road-tripping with them. Through our dollars and our recreational bent, we've created the only internationally known mountain bike destination: Moab, Utah, which answers the entire globe's Marlboro Country fantasies.

Of course, there's dirt all over the world. Great dirt. I fervently hope readers will search it out. The intent of this book is to celebrate mountain bike travel in general and to illuminate the charms of 21 destinations in particular. May you enjoy both the reads and the rides.

USING THE BOOK

Each chapter begins with an overview essay. These contain some hard information, but mostly serve to characterize the destination and illustrate why we enjoy riding there. After the essays

come a series of headings. Some are self-explanatory. The others are explained below.

AT A GLANCE

This section lists the vital statistics for each trip.

Trip Length. The minimal amount of time to spend riding in the area. This does not include travel time.

Physical Challenge. The physical demands of each trip are rated 1 through 5, with 1 being the easiest and 5 the hardest. The ratings reflect technical difficulty, roughness of terrain, altitude, and other factors. Destinations with 4 and 5 ratings will demand considerable mountain bike experience.

Mental Challenge. Also organized on a scale of 1 to 5, this category evaluates a destination's logistics. In other words, it accounts for anything that can confound traveling mountain bikers: language barriers, iffy hygiene, poorly marked trails, changing access regulations, unpredictable weather, and more.

Prime Time. The months with optimal mountain biking conditions. Note: crowds and prices can often decrease if you travel during off-prime time.

Price Range (independent trip). The beauty of mountain biking is that it can cost little once you get the gear. It's not like skiing, where you have to buy lift tickets. It's not like trekking in that it requires lots of pre-planning or guides. It's not like sea kayaking in that the equipment is so big and cumbersome that you want to rent often. Prices listed under this subheading will cover food, inexpensive lodging, and miscellaneous charges, but not bike rental or guiding services.

Price Range (outfitted group trip). Prices listed under this subhead reflect the cost of taking an organized trip with a reliable mtb outfitter. For multi-day trips, the price usually covers food, guiding, lodging, and bike rental. For day trips, the price usually covers guiding and lunch, but not always bike rental.

Staging City. Where to fly, either to best reach a destination or to commence a road trip.

Heads Up. Some destinations are safer than others: This category tells you what to beware of and when.

THE RIDES

These are recommendations for where to pedal and why. They do not qualify as trail guides, so you should still seek out advice from locals or consult a thorough guidebook or map. I trust I've supplied enough information that any mountain biker with any experience at all will be able to find the rides and have the groundwork that he or she can learn the nuts and bolts. I've supplied ride mileages where possible, but keep in mind that this book uses a fairly loose definition of "ride." Under this heading, I've listed trail networks, bike tours, entire state parks, and loops with lots of spurs and options. On many such "rides," the final mileage really depends on how far the rider wishes to ride.

Finally, a word on the book's organization. I've grouped the destinations into four categories:

The Meccas are those towns or small regions known among the mtb cognoscenti for their great—and abundant—rides. Along with fine dirt, Meccas boast first-rate shops, easily found trail information, and plentiful mtb culture.

The Tropics section describes already popular tourist destinations that happen to enjoy a great diversity of mtb opportunities—not to mention benevolent climates and swaying palms.

The Road Trips include all manner of destinations, some developed and some raw. Because their various rides are spread over a wide geographic area, they're best visited by driving a car from spot to spot.

The Outer Limits destinations represent mountain bike travel's cutting edge, where the rider will need to be independent, self-sufficient, and tolerant of Third World conditions.

Opposite: Biking on slickrock near Moab, Utah.
Overleaf: World-class mountain biker Hans Rey, Nu'alolo Trail, Na Pali Coast, Kauai, Hawaii.

Downieville & Nevada City

Mark Twain's rollicking Gold Country meets John Muir's beloved Sierra here, where precious veins of singletrack run beneath 100-foot conifers.

There are several reasons why the Downieville Downhill (DD) reigns as the globe's premier mountain bike ride. First off, its 17-mile length makes it one of the most prolonged descents you'll ever coast. Second, the DD spends most of its length as a thrilling, narrow ribbon of singletrack. Third, if your hands get sore from squeezing brakes, you can pull over and gaze at the breathtaking scenery of California's Gold Country.

And the Downieville Downhill is just one of many spectacular rides in this neck of the Sierra Nevada. The northern part of Gold Country, specifically Sierra and Yuba Counties, is simply ideal for riding. The mountains rise as much as 7,000 vertical feet above the valleys. Winter rains make the trails lush and plush, renewing them for the long, spring-to-fall riding season. The long, crystalline days of summer bring 80°F temperatures but little humidity. The mountains aren't

Racing the 17-mile-long Downieville Downhill.

CALIFORNIA

Downieville

Nevada City

Lake Tahoe

Sacramento

Sierra Nevada

overly steep, allowing trails to cross them at will—noodling over ridges and dropping into drainages.

The trails—more than 300 miles worth—wind between tall stands of ponderosa and sugar pines. Over soft dirt or carpets of needles. Along fern-lined water channels. Through fine, suspended curtains of dust. Around fat rocks and gnarled cedar roots. Under waving branches and blue sky. On narrow footbridges above churning water. The Gold Country ripples with an infinity of ridges, foothills, and peaks—preventing the establishment of roads, ranches, farms, or anything else that could interrupt a good long ride in the woods.

If mountain bike areas were rated like college entrance exams, Downieville–Nevada City would score in the 98th percentile. Whatever you value in a mountain bike trail—technical challenges, water crossings, smooth dirt, sinuous curves, beautiful views, lack of insects—you'll find it somewhere in the vicinity of Downieville.

For this bounty, mountain bikers can thank basic human greed. See, these trails weren't built by nature lovers such as John Muir—they were built by the California Gold Rush. The largest hard rock-mined gold nugget in America was pulled from Sierra County in 1853. It weighed a stunning 313 pounds. Miners began trampling through the woods, establishing paths that were pounded into permanence by pack mules.

The town of Downieville, which occupies a rare flat spot at the junction of the Downie and North Yuba Rivers, is the ideal base for anyone exploring these Sierra trails. At the height of the Gold Rush, this narrow strip of Victorian buildings had a population of 5,000. Now that the gold is gone, Downieville is home to only 350 residents. The town's economy is built on tourism, some from fly fishermen and some from travelers looking to cool off in the area's soothing aquamarine swimming holes (cyclists who are interested in such holes will find them easily on North and South Yuba Trails).

The town fathers are especially grateful for the recent influx of mountain bikers. Downieville is one small town where Lycra bike shorts don't get funny looks at the diner. Businesses zealously support the annual fat-tire festival. The local branch of the Forest Service is filled with rangers who advocate nonmotorized two-wheeled recreation—because they're riders themselves. Suffice it to say, trail access is not a problem around Downieville.

AT A GLANCE

TRIP LENGTH 6 days	PRICE RANGE (INDEPENDENT TRIP) $275
PHYSICAL CHALLENGE 1 2 3 ④ 5	PRICE RANGE (OUTFITTED GROUP TRIP) $600
MENTAL CHALLENGE 1 ② 3 4 5	STAGING CITY Sacramento, California
PRIME TIME May–October	HEADS UP Late summer often brings copious dust

Forty-five miles south of Downieville is the Gold Country's other mountain biking hub, Nevada City. A larger (population 2,855), more touristy Gold Rush town that regularly appears in commercials and Westerns, Nevada City clings to treacherous hillsides in piney woods. Its trails are every bit as superb as those in Downieville, only a little more spread out.

Muir's first trip to the area left him raving about "trees and stars, hushed by solemn-sounding waterfalls and many small soothing voices in sweet accord whispering peace!" My first trip produced somewhat less eloquent memories, but memories nonetheless. I'll never forget my riding buddy's exclamations of "...so nice, so nice..." like he was muttering sweet nothings to a favorite pet or speaking in tongues after some ecstatically spiritual experience.

WHAT TO EXPECT

Downieville and Nevada City are located northwest of Lake Tahoe on California Hwy. 49. Fly into either Reno or Sacramento. Reno is closer to

Riding along the Tamarack Lakes beneath the Sierra Buttes.

Downieville (about a 90-minute drive), while Sacramento is about an hour from Nevada City.

Weather during the summer and early fall is customarily ideal: warm, sunny days with little rain. Winter snows usually bury the trails of Downieville, but Nevada City sometimes boasts year-round riding. Spring can bring anything from snow to scorching heat. If winter and spring are dry, the trails can suffer from dustiness in late summer. You can get used to the looser traction, but you'll want to wear eye protection, especially if you ride with contact lenses.

You need to pay attention when you ride here. The narrowness of the trails can make them mentally exhausting, and many cling to steep cliffsides with serious exposure. One mistake—say, striking a rock with your pedal—can send you on a very painful if not downright hazardous tumble. If you question your aptitude at handling cliffs and big drop-offs, stick to the relatively flatter riverside trails.

Many of the best trails begin from high-mountain saddles. If you're not in fantastic shape,

LOW IMPACT

As mountain biking continues to flourish in the Gold Country, some other trail users have grumbled about cyclists' impact. To see if the complaints had any merit, the Forest Service undertook an erosion study before and after one of the Downieville Classic races. Rangers found that the 877 riders who raced caused as much soil damage as three—yep, three—dirt bikes.

Above: On Chimney Rock, one of Crested Butte's high-altitude trails.
Overleaf: Sunset from the Sierra Buttes, one of the rewards of riding up to 7,000-foot Packer Saddle.

or even if you are but don't like climbing uphill for-ever, consider arranging a shuttle (see Outfitters), especially for the Chimney Rock Trail and rides descending from the 7,000-foot Packer Saddle.

Local bike and outdoors stores sell topo maps that reveal the trails in hyper-detail, but you won't get lost if you just get a Gold Country Trail Guide from Yuba Expeditions (see Outfitters). The guide has capsule versions of topo maps and easy-to-follow, detailed instructions.

For general information, contact the Sierra County Visitors Bureau (800-720-7782) or the Chamber of Commerce in Downieville (530-289-3507) or Nevada City (530-265-2692).

<h3 align="center">LODGING</h3>

The Downieville River Inn and Resort (800-696-3308; www.downievilleriverinn.com) offers affordable rooms, as well as barbecue grills and a heated swimming pool.

For camping information, call the U.S. Forest Service (530-478-6253). Though the Sierra boasts

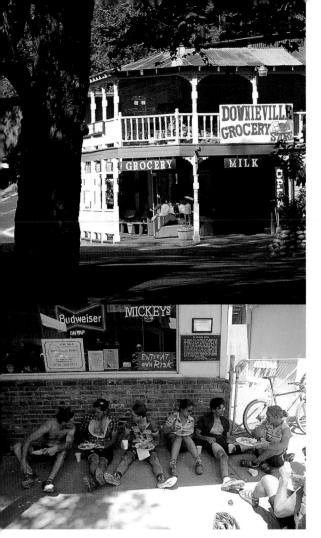

Top: Downieville Gocery Store.
Above: Common street scene in downtown Downieville.

near perfect camping conditions, the prices for organized facilities are expensive: $17 per night.

THE RIDES

Gold Country rides mix a variety of trail conditions. There are a few rutted fire roads, but most of the rides are on singletrack—all kinds of singletrack. Be prepared for smooth, velvety dirt; for riding in water on trails that actually double as streambeds; for a variety of rocks, including shale, which makes a musically clinking noise. Indeed, one local trail is nicknamed "The Money Trail" for its sonic resemblance to a cash register.

DOWNIEVILLE

The premier trail is the Downieville Downhill, which drops 5,000 vertical feet in 17 miles. It's essentially a three-trail linkage: Butcher Ranch to Third Divide to First Divide. The trail mixes tight switchbacks, fun jumps, and high-speed runs through 100-foot trees. Start at Packer Saddle and finish in town.

The North Yuba Trail is a roller coaster that undulates alongside the gorgeous North Yuba River. Start at Rocky Rest Campground a few miles west of Downieville and ride it either as an out-and-back or make it a more exerting 17-mile loop by going through the quaint town of Goodyear's Bar and connecting to the Fiddle Creek Ridge Trail.

Another classic route combines the Chimney Rock and Empire Creek trails. Shuttle to the Chimney Rock trailhead west of town, then climb along an above-timberline ridge offering great views of Mount Lassen and other huge volcanoes. Switchback down Empire Creek almost all the way to Downieville before picking up the First Divide trail.

NEVADA CITY

Around Nevada City, Bullards Bar is a must-ride. A 28-mile ride that contours around scenic Marysville Lake, Bullards boasts swooping downhill sections, which are pitched so ideally you hardly need to brake. And its flat and uphill sections are entertaining squiggles through the creekbeds that empty into the lake. Start at Sunset Vista Point, a few miles east of Nevada City, riding short stints on the 8-Ball and Rebel Ridge trails to get to Bullards Bar.

The South Yuba Primitive Camp Loop is famous for its pristine swimming holes. The loop starts at the South Yuba Primitive Camp and goes basically clockwise for 19 giddy miles.

PANNING FOR GOLD

The Gold Rush precipitated one of the largest migrations in human history. Panning for gold may seem like a hopeless anachronism, but lots of modern-day visitors to Gold Country try it—perhaps because a 160-pound nugget was found not too long ago in the North Yuba River. To strike it rich, swirl river dirt or sand around in a 12- to 15-inch pan till the dirty water and loose stuff spills out. You'll be left with heavier minerals called black sand. Check it for nuggets or specks that will change your life.

OUTFITTERS AND BIKE SHOPS

Yuba Expeditions pioneered many of the Gold Country trails and established the Downieville Classic race/festival. It offers tours, shuttles, rentals, and maps. Before you ride anything in Gold Country, call Yuba first.

For basic shops, try the Tour of Nevada City Bicycle Shop. In Downieville, try Downieville Outfitters.

YUBA EXPEDITIONS
P.O. Box 750
Nevada City, CA 95959
530-265-8779
www.yubaexpeditions.com
$45 per day

TOUR OF NEVADA CITY BICYCLE SHOP
457 Sacramento
Nevada City, CA 95959
530-265-2187

DOWNIEVILLE OUTFITTERS
P.O. Box 432
Downieville, CA 95936
530-289-0155
www.downievilleoutfitters.com
$45 per day

RECOMMENDED READING

■ *THE CELEBRATED JUMPING FROG OF CALAVERAS COUNTY*, Mark Twain (1965. $3.50. Filter Press.) Twain once wrote for and edited Downieville's *Mountain Messenger*, California's oldest weekly newspaper. His Gold Country days are perhaps best experienced in this story.
■ *MOUNTAIN BIKE!: NORTHERN CALIFORNIA*, Linda Gong Austin (2000. $15.95. Menasha Ridge Press.)

Crested Butte

Savor the alpine peaks and crystal blue mornings that inspired John Denver's "Rocky Mountain High."

At 9 A.M. on one of those crystal blue mornings that have made tourism one of Colorado's top industries since John Denver first sang "Rocky Mountain High," six of us pile out of our cars at a Crested Butte trailhead. We are at least an hour behind schedule thanks to a small misunderstanding about the rendezvous, a last-minute run to the grocery store for fruit and water, and the inevitable coffee-lubricated runs to the bathroom. Still, we brim with optimism at the trailhead. The sun is bright, and fat, friendly cumulus clouds float benignly as blimps across the horizon. In the Rocky Mountains, the cumulus are your friends, as they signify stable high pressure. We'll check the sky repeatedly to make sure the clouds don't degenerate into high, wispy cirrus, the precursor to blackening weather.

Chains are lubed, headsets checked, tires pumped. Everyone drifts into a line and begins pedaling at a strong pace. Within minutes, we're

Perfect puddle, near Kebler Pass, west of Crested Butte.

riding in precise order on a sinuous trail snaking past a photogenic old miner's cabin. The Colorado sunshine shimmers on the still-dewy grass. We wonder if we've somehow been beamed into a Coors Light commercial.

With the cumulus holding strong, we climb to a ridge. Below yawns a downhill singletrack. Blemished occasionally with roots and rocks, the trail is challenging, yet pitched at an angle that keeps us off the brakes and rolling fast. We nurse our wheels around tight corners, jam on the cranks for a few revolutions, then lay the tires on the sidewalls for the next smooth, flowing turn.

Mountain biking is a way of life in Crested Butte. Like spokes from a wheel, more than 900 miles of dirt roads and singletrack radiate out, in every direction, from Crested Butte into the surrounding Gunnison National Forest. Year-round, locals can be seen riding to work, riding to play, and just riding to roam atop their two-wheeled townies. The town is so gung ho on this form of alternative transportation, there's even a fleet of communal bikes available for people who need a quick lift around the historic 19th-century mining town. The "cow bikes"—so called because of the holstein-flavored paint job that identifies the bikes as loaners—are built and maintained by a group of local seventh graders and resident bike mechanics.

Along with Marin County, California, Crested Butte is recognized as the birthplace of mountain biking. Crested Butte hosts the Mountain Biking Hall of Fame, the sport's longest-running fat-tire festival, several frame-builders, and—most important to our way of thinking—the best high-altitude riding in the world.

The key to Crested Butte is its topography. Unlike most Colorado mountain towns that also double as ski resorts, Crested Butte doesn't occupy a narrow box canyon. Nor is it hemmed in by an interstate highway. Sure, Crested Butte boasts its share of jutting, 12,000-foot peaks. But it mixes them with sprawling valleys, rolling hills, and lush meadows. The result is a trail network that rarely gets too steep for mountain biking. In some Colorado towns the trails only drop and plummet; in Crested Butte, they also dip and meander.

Moreover, Crested Butte is beautiful. In summer, visitors can see every color in the rainbow—fitting, since Crested Butte landscapes frequently sport rainbows, even double rainbows. The town won designation as the Wildflower

AT A GLANCE

TRIP LENGTH 6 days	PRICE RANGE (INDEPENDENT TRIP) $400
PHYSICAL CHALLENGE 1 2 3 4 ⑤	PRICE RANGE (OUTFITTED GROUP TRIP) $1,000
MENTAL CHALLENGE 1 2 ③ 4 5	STAGING CITY Gunnison, Colorado
PRIME TIME June–September	HEADS UP Mountain weather always changing

ride, bar none. Aspens wear their branches high, so they rarely stab riders or interfere with forward progress. The aspen's fluttering round leaves filter sunlight into kaleidoscopic rays. Their distinctive pale bark makes the forest brighter. Crested Butte's Snodgrass Mountain, where the trees stand as tall and white and true as BYU basketball players, is an exemplary ride for exploring aspens. The trail snakes crazily back and forth; you can glance sideways and see that your riding partner is 20 feet away and pedaling in the opposite direction. The flashes of *rider-tree-rider-tree* tease the retinas like a strobe.

Crested Butte is surrounded by the Elk Mountains and three major wilderness areas. Its vistas are little cluttered by civilization. Riders enjoy a changing mix of woods, meadows, and above-timberline rock. And the trails can ramble at length: It's not uncommon for hardcores to put together rambling, 70-mile loops. The ability to connect different ribbons of trails into epics is what attracts endurance racers in the Leadville 100 to come to Crested Butte to train. Unless you're such an animal, you can bike for two weeks in Crested Butte and never repeat a ride.

In Crested Butte, riders don't often wrestle with the ethical dilemma of driving pollution-spewing cars to trailheads in order to practice an environmentally kind sport. Most of the prime trails are located just a short spin out of town. And Crested Butte is a fine place from which to plan your next epic. Incorporated in 1880, the town itself has been declared a National Historic District. Its well-preserved, late-19th-century architecture reflects its origins as a supply town for Colorado's gold and silver booms. When the precious metals ran out, the town turned to coal mining. Since the 1960s, tourism has supported Crested Butte. Visitors come for the recreation and the chance to breathe clear mountain air among brightly painted Victorian houses.

Top: In Crested Butte, muddy, grungy mountain bikers fit right in. Above: The town is surrounded by Gunnison National Forest and more than 900 miles of dirt roads and singletrack.

Capital of Colorado for its varied and often huge blooms. At the peak of wildflower season, riders sometimes struggle to see the trail. The overgrowth of flowers restricts sight lines to the narrow wake knifed open by your front wheel. To ride it, you let off the brakes, hang back of the saddle, and surf the billion petals like a wave.

Crested Butte also boasts many groves of aspen—in my book, the best species of trees to

Opposite: A downhill racer sails down one of the many dirt roads that crisscross Gunnison National Forest.

Crested Butte's flat meadows and riverside trails provide relief from its many long steep downhills.

Plus, Crested Butte is known for a free-wheeling attitude long thought to be extinct in a state where resorts sometimes seem overwhelmed by Hollywood-style glitz. Hippies remain a strong cultural influence. Pizza delivery drivers dodge quasi-feral dogs and complain about patchouli-oil-scented houses. Some locals live in crude shacks in the woods. Needless to say, muddy, grungy mountain bikers blend right in.

WHAT TO EXPECT

Crested Butte occupies a broad valley in south-central Colorado. Major airlines serve Gunnison, located 28 miles to the south on state Hwy. 135. If you drive, it's about a four-and-a-half hour trip from Denver. The town of Crested Butte sits three miles below the ski resort, Mount Crested Butte. Both the town and the resort present easy access to a variety of trails (most of them in the Gunnison National Forest). Because Crested Butte is such a well-established ski resort, it transitions easily into a mountain-bike resort—featuring many capable bike shops, a nice selection of restaurants, and all kinds of lodging opportunities.

Crested Butte belongs on anyone's "must-ride" list. The bike-worshipping town is a joy to stroll or pedal. The singletracks are as aesthetically perfect as the alpine vistas. The Mountain Bike Hall of Fame will impress you with Crested Butte's history and make you proud to ride. Even if you come during the annual mtb festival, you won't feel crowded. The size of the ski area, which has hosted the ESPN Winter X Games, spreads out the significantly smaller mtb crowds.

Crested Butte's alpine summers are short

and sometimes tough. Heavy winter snowfalls can keep some rides closed through June. Late summer brings afternoon storms, sometimes with hail. Always carry a rain jacket. September and early October occasionally bring the best riding imaginable: dry trails through groves of aspen turning gold. But early snowstorms can also strike.

For general information, contact the Crested Butte Visitors Bureau (800-545-4505) or the Crested Butte-Mount Crested Butte Chamber of Commerce (970-349-6438 or 800-545-4505; www.crestedbuttechamber.com). For camping and trails information, call the Gunnison National Forest (970-641-0471).

LODGING

The Claim Jumper Inn Bed & Breakfast (970-349-6471; claimjumper@visitcrestedbutte.com) is a prototypical Crested Butte place to bunk: an historic log home with six uniquely decorated theme rooms (one festooned just with Coca-Cola memorabilia) that allows bikers and dogs.

Budget travelers will gravitate to the Forest Queen (970-349-5336 or 800-937-1788; forest@crestedbutte.net). Built in 1881, the "Queen" was a bar during the town's early years, and is reported to have been part of the red-light district. Today, it's a restaurant and hotel known for good grub and reasonably priced accommodations.

THE RIDES

Expert riders relish Crested Butte, but beginners may not. The town sits 9,000 feet above sea level, and the altitude can punish the small-lunged. The climbs are harsh, requiring stamina, balance, and a serious set of guts to keep on grunting when the lack of oxygen and the surplus of gravity invites you to dismount. The ascents can climb as much as 4,000 vertical feet. The downhills are often long and steep; your hands may get fried from constantly squeezing the brakes. Whenever the mountains begin to crush you, though, Crested Butte's somewhat flat meadows and riverside trails provide needed relief.

Trail 401 is one of several fine Crested Butte trails that begin with nondescript numbers. Try

THE LEGEND OF NEIL MURDOCH

Crested Butte riders speak reverently about a man known as Neil Murdoch. Murdoch was hugely prominent in Crested Butte's mountain biking circles. He pioneered the first Pearl Pass tour to Aspen in 1976, a watershed moment in the sport. He started Crested Butte's Fat Tire Bike Week, the first major mtb festival. For his contributions, Murdoch became an original inductee into the Mountain Bike Hall of Fame. But it turns out that Murdoch wasn't Murdoch at all: He was Richard Bannister, a fugitive from the law who had eluded a nationwide manhunt for 25 years. Bannister was originally arrested in 1973 on charges of importing 26 pounds of cocaine with intent to distribute. He posted bond, but never showed up for his court date. Instead, he fled to the end-of-the-road town of Crested Butte. He became active, as Neil Murdoch, in local politics and theater. But when he used someone else's social security number on credit applications in 1988, U.S. marshals came to check on him. They eventually pieced out "Murdoch's" true identity, and the FBI prepared to arrest him. But the wily Bannister escaped again. He convinced a friend to drive him to the Utah desert. The friend dropped him off, and Neil Murdoch/Richard Bannister mountain biked off into the red rock without a trace.

Speeding through a grove of aspens on the race course just off Trail 401, Mount Crested Butte.

high wildflowers and skunk cabbage.

Reno/Flag/Bear/Deadman's entails 22 miles and 2,700 feet of cumulative elevation gain—plus copious amounts of both challenge and bliss. The route links the Reno Divide, Flag, and Bear Creek trails. Big climbs lead to screaming downhills and, for the finale, a serpentine descent down 28 switchbacks into Deadman's Gulch.

Pearl Pass is the classic, historic mountain bike ride that connects Crested Butte with Aspen, traversing sensational backcountry on high-elevation terrain. The route is most spectacular on the south side of the Elk Range; so many riders try an out-and-back ride to the top of the pass, beginning and ending in Crested Butte.

OUTFITTERS AND BIKE SHOPS

The World Outside, a Colorado-based outfitter, offers a trip called the Crested Butte Singletracker that boasts "smooth singletrack trails through meadows of wildflowers, thrilling descents from the rooftop of the Rockies, and fun and fast curves through aspen forests." *Bicycling* magazine rated it one of the "50 Best Trips on the Planet."

Of the many fine shops in Crested Butte, the Alpineer is the most venerable. Open since 1969, the Alpineer has aided the Butte's mtb passions since the beginning. When you buy something from the Alpineer, it disburses 1 percent of the money to preservation of open space.

THE WORLD OUTSIDE
2840 Wilderness Place, #F
Boulder, CO 80301
800-488-8483 / 303-413-0938
www.theworldoutside.com
$910 for 6 days
THE ALPINEER
419 6th St.
Crested Butte, CO 81224
970-349-5120
www.alpineer.com

403 and 409 as well as 401, a true test of bike handling while running an exposed narrow ridge line along the Maroon Bells Wilderness boundary. After a healthy ascent that crests to a panoramic view of the Bells, the 401 begins a long, rolling descent with many switchbacks through shoulder-

Ideal day for a ride, Kebler Pass (9,980 feet), just west of Crested Butte.

RECOMMENDED READING

■ To scope the trails, check the *ASPEN-CRESTED BUTTE-GUNNISON RECREATION TOPO MAP* from Latitude 40 Degrees, Inc. (303-258-7909).
■ For general guidebooks that include Crested Butte, get *COLORADO GONZO RIDES: A MOUNTAIN BIKER'S GUIDE TO COLORADO'S BEST SINGLE TRACK TRAILS,* Michael Merrifield (1991. $12.95. Blue Clover Press.)

■ *CENTENNIAL,* James A. Michener (1994. $7.00. Fawcett.) A story of trappers, traders, homesteaders, gold seekers, ranchers, and hunters— all caught up in the dramatic events and violent conflicts that shaped the destiny of our legendary West. Set in the fictional town of Centennial, Colorado, the book speaks to anyone who tolerates the hassles and thin air of a place like Crested Butte in order to spend time on the raw, beautiful shoulders of the Rockies.

Durango

In the hotbed of mountain bike racing, the sport is a civic cause. Even the greasy spoons are decorated with autographed pictures of famous mtb competitors.

Photographer David Wilkins and I had just made our way back to Wilkins' Durango home from a ride to remember. We'd spent four hours gliding sinuous trails in crisp October air. While the dry, traction-friendly dirt unspooled beneath our tires, we peered at a cloudless cerulean sky through a golden canopy of twirling aspen leaves. Neither of us suffered a mechanical. I underwent two unintentional dismounts, but saw them coming early enough to fend off

serious corporal damage. An all-time top-10 ride? Maybe. Definitely a refreshing reminder as to why one mountain bikes instead of jogs.

Ensconced on Wilkins' front porch with cold beers from a local microbrewery in hand, we chatted about the ride while soaking up the amber light of a warm October afternoon. I don't know if it was the beer, the amber light, or general post-ride euphoria, but I gushed some vague sentiment about how the Four Corners

Another traction-friendly dirt singletrack threads along a mesa overlooking Durango, southwest Colorado.

area of America boasts seemingly ideal conditions for riding mountain bikes.

Wilkins, a laconic sort, didn't speak for a moment. Then he nodded at the landscape before us. I followed his gaze past the two-lane artery buzzing with bike-rack-equipped Subaru station wagons, past the bright yellow aspens and rust shrub oak lining the floor of the Animas River Valley, and up to seven distinct mesas turning peach and rosy pink in the flattering light. "What I like about Durango," Wilkins said, "is that every mesa you see has mountain bike trails on it. And so do the mountains you don't see." I stared at all the lines crosshatching the mesas and nodded in agreement, glad that my fuzzy, inarticulate appreciation for Durango was supported by happy fact and compelling visual evidence.

Game trails have probably laced Durango's semiarid mesas since long before human habitation. Then, when white settlers came to this picturesque part of southwest Colorado in the 1880s, they quickly began cutting paths high into the peaks and mesas. The settlers were silver and gold prospectors, see, and their old pack trails were pitched for mules hauling heavy equipment. They tend to switchback up slopes and contour through drainages. The result is an ideal trail network for nonmotorized exploration.

But Durango boasts plenty of steep trails, too. For every gentle spin up a smooth fire road there's a molar-rattling plunge down a rock-choked chute. One in-town ride, Animas City Mountain, climbs 1,500 feet in two miles—a punishment so renowned in mtb circles that bike magazines journey there to put new designs to the test.

In 6,500-foot-high Durango, where the alpine grandeur of the San Juan Mountains melts abruptly into expansive red rock deserts, no single trail descriptor applies. Sure, the higher elevations boast plenty of classic Colorado singletrack—18-inch-wide ribbons of tacky dirt where knifing your handlebars between apertures of aspen trees sometimes requires divine blessing and a well-timed shrug. Lower down are rolling sandy washes festooned with juniper bushes. Durangoans can get in a good sweat there during their lunch break while their pals toil on one of the area's several "epics"—70-plus-mile routes that rise to the marmot-ruled no-man's-land above timberline.

Rocky Mountains

Continental Divide

Denver

I-70

COLORADO

San Juan National Forest

San Juan Mountains

●Durango

NEW MEXICO

AT A GLANCE

TRIP LENGTH 5 days   PRICE RANGE (INDEPENDENT TRIP) $250

PHYSICAL CHALLENGE 1 2 ③ 4 5   PRICE RANGE (OUTFITTED GROUP TRIP) $600

MENTAL CHALLENGE ① 2 3 4 5   STAGING CITY Durango, Colorado

PRIME TIME April–October   HEADS UP Hunting season (October) demands bright clothing, extra precautions

Mtb champion John Tomac and family. Tomac and several other world-class competitors have made Durango home.

Ask any local why he rides Durango and the word "variety" will inevitably spill over his lips. Durango guidebooks describe more than 40 rides in the immediate vicinity. Spend a month riding here, and you still won't be bored. Moreover, you can pedal to most trails right from charming Victorian downtown Durango.

The combination of superb selection and easy accessibility remained largely a secret until 1990, when Durango hosted the inaugural World Mountain Bike Championships. Suffice it to say, none of the racers questioned Durango's world-class credentials. Indeed, many of them soon returned with moving trucks. The local trails, combined with Durango's long riding season and benevolent climate (300 sunny days per year), make it an optimal place for pros to train and for the rest of us to ride.

World mtb champions such as Ned Overend, Missy Giove, Juli Furtado, John Tomac, and Greg Herbold have all lived in Durango at one point or another. Even if these names mean nothing to you, even if you view racing as a misguided attempt to turn a meditative outdoors experience into a furious competition, you'll benefit from Durango's racing heritage. Thanks to the World Championships, the annual Iron Horse Classic race, and the presence of dozens of pros, Durango caters to mountain bike interests as much as any town in America. Bike shops, staffed with crack mechanics, abound. Restaurants understand that carbo loading can, and should, transcend spaghetti and Ragu. You never have to search for a place to lock your rig. Even the greasy spoons are decorated with autographed pictures of famous riders.

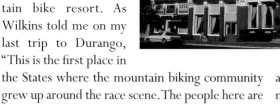

Durango is a college town, a county seat, and a diverse city of 12,430 people. Yet it often feels like a mountain bike resort. As Wilkins told me on my last trip to Durango, "This is the first place in the States where the mountain biking community grew up around the race scene. The people here are still proud of that. In Durango, mountain biking is a civic cause."

WHAT TO EXPECT

Durango is located in southwest Colorado, 380 miles southwest of Denver and about 30 miles east of Mesa Verde National Park on U.S. Hwy. 160. The city's airport is served by major airlines, with direct flights from Phoenix and Denver.

Again, most trails are easily reached from Durango proper. You may, however, want shuttle capability: Getting to the trailheads of the long rides north of town can entail five hours of circuitous pedaling, much of it on pavement. In other words, you could possibly suffer a day-ending mechanical before you even reach the dirt.

The sheer number of trails does a good job of spreading out riders, but you can experience crowds on weekends during the high season of summer and fall. Popular multiuse trails such as Hermosa Creek can contain hikers, horseback riders, hunters, other cyclists, and even motorcycles (which are legal there). The screaming downhill singletrack beckons, but watch those blind curves.

Durango's riding season usually stretches from April through November. In-town trails can be rideable in winter, but don't count on it. Spring combines long days with occasional snow remnants in shaded sections. Summer heralds the opening of the long, high-altitude rides. It also brings some of the craziest weather: sometimes uncomfortable heat in town and frequent afternoon thunderstorms. On high country rides, no matter how sunny it is when you depart, bring a waterproof shell. Autumn is perhaps the best time to ride: The crisp, invigorating temperatures are rarely accompanied by precipitation. But you do need to watch for big game hunters starting in October, so wear your brightest clothes.

For general information, contact the Durango Area Chamber Resort Association (800-463-8726) or the San Juan National Forest (970-247-4874).

LODGING

Located in downtown Durango, The Best Western Rio Grande Inn (800-245-4466; Info@BWRioGrandeInn.com) lies just a short walk from the region's biggest tourist attraction: the Durango and Silverton Narrow Gauge Railroad. The Riverhouse Bed and Breakfast (800-254-4775; Info@Durango-Riverhouse.com) sits closer to the trailhead of Durango's best-loved trail, Hermosa Creek.

The Strater Hotel, Main Street, Durango (population 12,430). The town is home of the annual Iron Horse Classic mtb race.

WHOA, BESSIE!

In 1990, just before the World Champion-ships, the employees at Purgatory Resort had to round up a wayward cow that had been wandering around the ski mountain for weeks. Fortunately, the cow was contained before the races, and no rider was faced with a bovine collision while rolling 30 miles-per-hour down the Worlds course.

THE RIDES

Durango rides are at times blissfully effortless. Generally speaking, riders are not annoyed by excessive rocks, roots, mud, thorns, or mosquitos. However, many trails do involve cliffside exposures, and above-timberline rides can subject you to dangerous lightning storms. Altitude is also a concern, with some trails soaring as high as 11,000 feet. The usual advice—get in shape and drink plenty of water—definitely applies.

Durango represents the southwestern terminus of the Colorado Trail (CT), which winds from Denver through 480 miles worth of mountains. The CT contains many Wilderness Area sections, which are illegal to ride, but the sublime stretch from Molas Pass (47 miles north of town) to Durango is completely legal. Typical of trails north of the city, Molas to Durango is comprised mostly of singletrack. Truly gonzo riders can pedal this winding, 70-plus-mile route in a day. But it's more fun to stretch it to three or four days and camp; either hire an outfitter or take turns driving a support vehicle. (The Telluride to Durango ride begins west of Molas Pass, but later connects to the same lower portions of the CT.)

Hermosa Creek Trail is 21 miles of slightly to moderately technical singletrack leading from meadows surrounded by aspens and blue spruce, along a rushing creek, through forests of pines, to the edge of the high desert. There are some steep hillside traverses and some steep sections of the trail that many riders will choose to walk. But generally the trail is downhill for its entire length. If you can be dropped off, start the trail at its upper end at the junction of Hermosa Creek and Road # 578 from Purgatory Ski Resort. You will end the trip at a dirt/paved road just north of the village of Hermosa, which is a few easy miles north of Durango.

Like Hermosa Creek, Jones Creek is one of many trails dropping off the Hermosa Cliffs north of town. Its trailhead sits above the hamlet of Trimble. A singletrack that rolls through glades of aspen, Jones is fun just as an out-and-back. But it also connects to what Wilkins brags are "dozens of different loops you can do between Purgatory Ski Area and Durango."

Animas City Mountain is a horseshoe-shaped massif covered with a conifer and oak-brush forest. It's steep to climb and to descend, but from its top riders are rewarded with a sweeping view of the Animas River valley and of hundreds of miles of forested ridges and jagged peaks.

Purgatory's summer bike program continues to grow, and the resort offers inexpensive lift rides, mountain bike rentals, and a trail map detailing an additional half-dozen rides for all abilities. In summer, the mixed spruce and aspen forests are alive with birds and animals, and the meadows are ablaze with wildflowers and cool, green grasses.

On the singletrack at the test trails on the edge of Durango.

The mesas surrounding Durango offer hundreds of miles of thrilling singletrack close to town.

OUTFITTERS AND BIKE SHOPS

For all manner of guided tours, contact local racer Dave Hegen, director of Durango Singletrack Tours. Western Spirit Cycling, a large outfit that runs tours all over the West, runs fully supported tours, including the sublime Telluride to Durango epic. Another Durango service: a mountain bike skills camp conducted by collegiate mtb legend Keith Darner (877-267-3622).

As for wrenching, Mountain Bike Specialists is considered the premier shop; it's certainly the biggest. Durango Cyclery and Hassle Free Sports are also well respected.

DURANGO SINGLETRACK TOURS
P.O. Box 3351
Durango, CO 81302
888-336-8687
$625 for 4 days

WESTERN SPIRIT CYCLING
478 Mill Creek Dr.
Moab, UT 84532
800-845-2453, 435-259-8732
www.westernspirit.com
$795 for 5 days

MOUNTAIN BIKE SPECIALISTS
949 Main Ave.
Durango, CO 81301
970-247-4066

DURANGO CYCLERY
143 E. 13th St.
Durango, CO 81301
970-247-0747

HASSLE FREE SPORTS
2615 Main Ave.
Durango, CO 81301
970-259-3874

RECOMMENDED READING

■ *DISCOVERIES*, Kent Nelson (1998. $16.95. Western Reflections Inc.) A collection of short stories set in the San Juans, *Discoveries* addresses the mountains' powerful influence on those who live within or travel through their austere and imposing beauty. The book's characters interact with the mountains in ways that are sometimes subtle, sometimes violent, but always profound. Riders who've pedaled a

The higher elevations, up in the San Juans, offer classic Colorado singletrack: 18-inch-wide ribbons of tacky dirt.

Durango mesa in the late afternoon's "golden hour" will recognize well-told moments like the following: "The elk ascend the last pitch to the saddle, and in the angle of the sun become part light and part silhouette as they disappear over the pass."

- *MOUNTAIN BIKING DURANGO* (1998. $10.95. Falcon.) A clear, concise guidebook.
- The *TRAILS ILLUSTRATED TOPO MAP: DURANGO,* sold at several shops, is quite good.

Hood River

Windsurfing still dominates the leisure pursuits in the Columbia River Gorge. If you sometimes feel a bit second-class as a rider, rest assured the trails are first-class.

More than anything else, Hood River is a community. Headquartered in the Oregon city of Hood River but by no means limited to it, the outdoor recreation community spreads west and east to towns on both the Oregon and the Washington sides of the Columbia River Gorge.

Arrive here with a bike, board, or kayak strapped to the rack, and you might just get sucked into this community without any warning.

If you don't watch out, innocently meeting a friend at the North Shore Alehouse across the river in Bingen, Washington, might lead to a re-creation of that opening scene in *Schindler's List*, where one by one every table in the place gets pulled together, and a room full of strangers is suddenly one massive organism of fun. As you move down the street to snarf Mexican at Fidel's, you talk about biking, about boarding, about wind and precipitation until you're throwing out terms

Jumping a fence near Hood River.

like "rain shadow" and "Coriolus effect" like you actually know what you're talking about. Next you find yourself winding along WA 14 above the banks of the Columbia, then corkscrewing up a mountain road to the weekend retreat of a Portland lawyer. You grab a sleeping bag from your car, crash on the outdoor deck, and wake up to an impulsive potluck breakfast, where everyone's raiding his cooler for something to throw into the most random, but quite possibly most exquisite, batch of scrambled eggs you've ever sampled. You make a contribution with a loaf of sourdough and the otherworldly blueberry jam you picked up at one of Oregon's roadside stands, and the resultant acclaim makes you feel like you're part of Hood River's supremely friendly and active community.

It's only when you suggest breaking out the bikes that you feel a sense of not belonging. Because even though the area's biking couldn't be better, everybody else puts off the idea of riding in order to go inside and cluster around a radio. And listen to the wind report. See, your new buddies might have bikes on their racks, they might love biking, they might excel at biking. But as my friend Lon said, Yoda-like, "If the wind is blowing, biking I am not going." Any thoughts you had on

the relative equality of sports pursuits in the area are dashed. Windsurfing is king. It's a rich irony. In a place where the mountain biking terrain, scenery, variety, accessibility, and acceptance are superior in all respects, the sport actually suffers from an inferiority complex.

While you sometimes feel a bit second-class as a rider here, the trails are first-class. Part of what makes Hood River such a dynamic place to ride is its location. Situated at the confluence of the Hood River and the mighty Columbia, the town is at ground zero when it comes to geological phenomena. The most striking feature is the Columbia River Gorge itself. It stretches more than 70 miles in length, is cut between rugged basalt cliffs that tower more than 4,000 feet above the river, and is home to more than 77 waterfalls on the Oregon side alone. Hood River is located in the center of the gorge, and experiences markedly different weather from the areas on either end. To the west, Oneonta Gorge supports a temperate rain forest that receives more than 75 inches of rain per year. At the east end, the town of Biggs in the high desert grassland commonly

Overleaf: Vista House, Columbia River Gorge National Scenic Area. Basalt cliffs rise 4,000 feet above the river.

AT A GLANCE

TRIP LENGTH 6 days	PRICE RANGE (INDEPENDENT TRIP) $300
PHYSICAL CHALLENGE 1 2 ③ 4 5	PRICE RANGE (OUTFITTED GROUP TRIP) $700
MENTAL CHALLENGE ① 2 3 4 5	STAGING CITY Portland, Oregon
PRIME TIME March–November	HEADS UP Heavy winter storms clutter trails with deadfall in spring

takes in only 12 inches annually. You virtually control the climate you're experiencing simply by travelling east or west through the gorge.

The landscape of the Hood River Valley can't match the gorge's climatic fluctuations, but its scenery is no less spectacular. The Hood River tumbles north past wildflower-adorned meadows, by thick timber stands, and under the shadow of impressive, bikeable ridges. The soil of the valley is full of volcanic minerals, and is an especially fertile place for fruit trees. Apples and peaches are transcendent, but pears are king. One-third of all the winter pears grown in the United States come from this area. Growers say that the warm days and cool nights of the growing season result in apples and pears that are astoundingly full-flavored and crisp. Stop by a roadside stand after a ride and sample some, and you'll be hard-pressed (no fruit pun intended) to disagree. Huckleberry season, which begins around Labor Day, brings numerous celebrations, and it's no wonder why. Fresh huckleberries make for nearly perfect finger food to bring on bike rides.

The blossoms of fruit trees lend color to an otherwise pretty valley, but the real scenic attraction is 11,235-foot Mount Hood, the striking, solitary, snowcapped volcanic peak of the Cascade Mountain Range. Mount Hood commands your attention no matter where you might be riding. The experience of arcing around a corner and coming into sudden view of Mount Hood is one you'll long remember. Even when you tell yourself that it's just a mountain peak, you find yourself drawn to staring at it. Resistance is futile. Even guidebook publishers, who should know better, can't help but focus on the peak. A chapter about Hood River in *Mountain Bike! Oregon* features write-ups of the numerous and varied trails in the area. Five of seven drastically different rides are accompanied by pictures of Mount Hood. You'll likely feel similarly mesmerized by the sight of the peak.

It's a sure bet that your eyes will catch sight of Mount Hood as frequently as your ears will pick up the phrase "transportation corridor" to describe what the Columbia River Gorge is to the area. The gorge serves as the only sea-level

Above: Downtown Hood River, at the midpoint of the 70-mile-long gorge.
Opposite: Cycling on the Rowena Loops, Historic Columbia River Highway.

WHAT'S THAT NOISE?

When the Lewis and Clark expedition traveled through the area in the early 1800s, the expedition's chief ornithologist John Townsend noted that the group had difficulty sleeping at night because the many birds in the area were so loud. Today, you'll still be struck by the size of the area's avian population, but the sound you'll really marvel at is the thunder of waterfalls. The Columbia River Gorge National Scenic Area has the world's highest concentration of tall waterfalls, with 77 cascades on the Oregon side alone.

Short carry, near Mount Hood. The western end of the Gorge receives 75 inches of rain annually.

WHAT TO EXPECT

Hood River is located 55 miles east of Portland International Airport on I-84, which runs along the Oregon side of the Columbia River. On the north bank, WA 14 connects the towns and trails of Washington.

Expect to feel a bit out of place as a mountain biker. That's not to say that the community is against us; far from it. But biking definitely takes second place to windsurfing in the area. Suggest going on a bike ride to your buddies on a day when the wind is blowing, and you'll feel like a blasphemer in the temple. Fortunately, if you do go biking on a good wind day, it's like cross-country skiing around a ski resort's golf course during a powder day: you'll enjoy a lot of solitude.

The terrain and climate surrounding Hood River make for exceptional biking. When the snow is still heavy in the mountains and the west end of the gorge is sodden with rain, head east for some early season spinning on the Deschutes River State Park Bike Path (dirt, not asphalt) in the high desert grasslands. Then, when spring and summer come to Hood River, check out the trails closer to home, such as Post Canyon and Surveyor's Ridge. On the hottest days, stay cool in the high elevation shade of Larch Mountain, or head to the Nestor Peak/Buck Creek area and a postride dip in Northwestern Lake. Riding Lewis River Trail in late summer or early fall is nothing short of spectacular.

There is an abundance of post-ride activities. There's nothing like finishing up a ride with a dip in the Columbia at Rooster Rock State Park or tossing a disc at the little city park in Bingen. You'll find all sorts of stores, cafes, and taverns in Hood River and the other towns along the river, and the music scene is surprisingly diverse.

While riding here, you'll easily forget that the big metropolis of Portland is less than an hour away via a convenient interstate highway. But

passage through the towering Cascades, and as such has historically provided a way for Native American traders, the Lewis and Clark expedition, and pioneers along the River Route of the Oregon Trail to travel to the Pacific Ocean. At present, cargo ships on the river, trains on tracks on both the Washington and Oregon banks, and trucks along busy I-84 use the transportation corridor as the most efficient route to get where they need to go. As a mountain biker, your mission is different: Your job is to find the most fun routes to travel, not the easiest.

Don't worry. You've come to the right place.

Bike camping near Hood River: double-checking the quick-release tension before heading out.

Portland's criminal class hasn't. U.S. Forest Service officials even had to close Palmer Mountain Road in the Columbia River Gorge National Scenic Area because gang members from Portland were using it as access to actually cut down trees with automatic weapon fire. More commonly, thieves target automobiles parked at trailheads. Break-ins are especially prevalent near the crowd-drawing waterfalls. Even if you're parked in a remote forest, don't leave valuables in plain sight, and secure all sports equipment as well as possible.

You might do some stealing yourself, however. While riding here, you can't help but sneak glances at the spectacular scenery, which ranges from the 4,000-foot basalt cliffs lining the

On Forest Service Road 44 near Surveyor's Ridge Trail, with Mount Hood's familiar profile.

find a great deal of general information by logging on to www.gorge.net. For more information on the public lands in the area, contact the Columbia River Gorge National Scenic Area (541-386-2333, www.fs.fed.us/r6/columbia) or Mount Hood National Forest, Hood River Ranger Station (541-352-6002, www.fs.fed.us/r6/mthood).

Check out Gorge Velo, a bicycling club that energetically promotes biking in the area, at www.gorgevelo.com

LODGING

Hood River Hotel (541-386-1900 or 800-386-1859; www.HoodRiverHotel.com) is a near anomaly: a historic inn oozing with charm that actually welcomes outdoor enthusiasts. It's located in downtown Hood River, close to bike shops and restaurants.

The gorge area is laced with state park, national forest, and municipal campgrounds. Contact the Columbia River Gorge National Scenic Area (541-386-2333 or www.fs.fed.us/r6/columbia for more information).

THE RIDES

Riding conditions vary tremendously. Some areas have exposed slate trails, some have good traction on volcanic soils, and places like Larch Mountain offer mud and cushiony pine needles in equal amounts. Singletrack trails are abundant, and access to them is very good. Keep it that way by riding responsibly and staying off the trails immediately after rains. You might have fun going mudding, but it's no fun for trail users who follow you to deal with the ruts you leave behind.

The favorite town ride is Post Canyon, located just a couple of miles from downtown Hood River. The network of wooded trails gets a lot of use (and shows it) but its myriad streams, abruptly appearing bridges, and slalom course of spruce and fir makes for energizing biking.

Surveyor's Ridge Trail, located in Hood

Columbia River Gorge, to the striking snow-capped summit of Mount Hood, to the wild-flowers adorning the area's ridges and plateaus. Don't forget to bring a camera.

For lodging, food, and shopping in Hood River, check out Hood River County Chamber of Commerce and Information Center (405 Portway Avenue, Hood River, OR 97031, 541-386-2000, 1-800-366-3530, www.gorge.net/hrccc). You can

River National Forest about 30 miles from town, winds through meadows and thick forest before emerging onto a ridge offering spectacular views of Hood River Valley. It's fun to be the first in a pack and hear the startled "Whoas" coming from your friends when they leave the trees and first lay eyes on Mount Hood across the valley. As if the distant views weren't enough, the ridgetop wildflowers are mesmerizing and the singletrack is mostly smooth and curvy. Nearby trails such as Dog River, Knebal Springs, Eightmile Loop, Fifteenmile Creek, and Gunsight are almost as memorable.

The Larch Mountain Loop, a network of singletrack trails perched high in the damp western portion of the gorge, offers some exciting plunges and climbs in amazingly lush forest. It can be bumpy and rooty, but the surroundings are so green and mossy and the trail surface so loamy that you somehow get the feeling that any falls you suffer will be softly cushioned. As a result, you find yourself braving technical challenges you might otherwise avoid. The only annoying thing about this ride is that you have the unshakeable feeling that if only the trees would recede a bit, your views would be awesome. Here's the cure: After you wrap up the ride, take a quick stroll up the stairway to Sherrard Point. On a clear day, you can line up the major peaks of the North Cascades: Mount Rainier, Mount Saint Helens, Mount Adams, Mount Hood, and Mount Jefferson are all clearly visible.

Lewis River Trail was considered one of the premier rides in the Northwest before the mid-1990s, when it got pummeled by winter storms. It's a judgment call whether the trail is as good as it once was, but you have to be a pretty spoiled rider not to be impressed by its friendly riding surface and gobsmacking views of Lewis River, waterfalls, and rock formations. It's an hour's drive from Hood River, but the car ride will vanish eons before your memories will. (Call Gifford Pinchot National Forest for current conditions, 360-891-5000.)

OUTFITTERS AND BIKE SHOPS

For a friendly, knowledgeable bike shop, head to Discover Bicycles. Seventh Sense Adventure Co. offers multisport trips that include Hood River mountain biking.

DISCOVER BICYCLES

205 Oak Street
Hood River, OR
541-386-4820
www.discoverbicycles.com

SEVENTH SENSE ADVENTURE CO.

877-330-0296
www.7thsenseadventure.com
$1,995 for 5 days

RECOMMENDED READING

Relevant guidebooks include:
- THE SINGLETRACK ANTHOLOGY, HOOD RIVER, Tyler Barnes and Kent Reynolds (1996. $10.95. HR Publishing.)
- MOUNTAIN BIKE! WASHINGTON, Alan Bennett and Chris & Laurie Leman (1998. $15.95. Menasha Ridge Press.)
- MOUNTAIN BIKE! OREGON, Chris & Laurie Leman (1998. $15.95. Menasha Ridge Press.)
- BICYCLING AMERICA'S NATIONAL PARKS: OREGON AND WASHINGTON, David Story (2001. $17.95. Countryman Press.)
- GREAT RIVER OF THE WEST: ESSAYS ON THE COLUMBIA RIVER, William L. Lang and Robert C. Carriker, editors (1999. $18.95. University of Washington Press.) The essays offer an illuminating look at the geological and cultural history of the area.

Moab

Singletrack, slickrock, chest-heaving uphills, ultra-technical downhills, and views that, if you weren't wearing a helmet, would blow the brains right out of your skull.

M oab, Utah, is far and away the most famous mountain bike destination in the world. Riders who don't call it Mecca, probably call it the Center of the Universe.

But what does this hype mean? What's Moab all about?

A day in Moab is about: Waking up in a sky-colored tent made bluer by the early morning sunshine creeping down the walls of the Colorado River canyon. Consciousness soon including the sounds of the river and the snoring of your still-tired riding partner.

Peeing in the cattails while regarding the fresh morning light bathing cathedrals of red rock. Toodling into Moab proper, passing the springs in the canyon walls where the thirsty fill jugs full of clear, cold life force. Finding the way to Mondo Café, and plunging into a steaming cup of even more necessary life force. A couple of bagels and muffins later, moving over to the visi-

Hitting—or taking off from—Moab's famous slickrock. The possibilities are limitless.

Salt Lake City

UTAH

to Grand Junction ➤
Moab
Canyonlands
National Park

Colorado River

tors center for the daily sponge bath. Saying, for the third straight day, "I'll shower tomorrow."

Riding over to the Poison Spider/Portal Trail. Finding singletrack, slickrock, chest-heaving uphills, ultra-technical downhills, and views that, if you weren't wearing a helmet, would blow the brains right out of your skull. Experiencing a good portion of our sport's sundry pleasures in a single session.

Finishing the ride and deciding a shower is not such a bad idea after all. Making your way to the youth hostel on the south side of town, where you can take a long, hot cleansing for only two bucks. Meeting a wild-eyed Australian there who tells you about the sketchy, unmarked, portage trail that peels off of Amasa Back trail and drops down to the John Wayne fantasyland of Jackson Hole. Vowing over a sweating can of Fosters Lager to do that very thing.

Buying *Desert Solitaire* at the bookstore. Carbo loading at Eddie McStiff's microbrewery, knowing your campstove remains lonely and unused in the back of the car. Returning to the tent, where you actually do some cooking over the campfire. Declaring to all who will listen that you are the Supreme Marshmallow Toasting Master of the Universe.

Crawling into the tent, feeling happy that there's a place where mountain bikers are welcomed and the rides are stunning, not giving a damn if the place is overexposed and overhyped. Because under the stars on the banks of the Colorado, it's not.

And that's just one day—in a place where you could easily spend a month. Between the La Sal Mountains that loom to the east and the untold basins and canyons pocking the Colorado Plateau, there are hundreds of miles of mountain bike-worthy dirt.

But dirt happens all over the world. Other mtb meccas have dirt. Only Moab strings bike trails along ancient ramparts of red stone.

Consider the Slickrock Trail, arguably the most famous mountain bike trail in the world. The Navajo sandstone surface is smooth, but not actually slick; mtb tires cling to it like cheese to pizza. On your first Slickrock uphill, you'll be startled by the traction. Accept it, believe in it. You can clear Slickrock's obstacles—the nearly vertical walls, concave dips, and half-pipe gullies—once you learn to keep pedaling. Riders who make the appropriate technique adjustments—hanging the butt and most internal organs over the rear knobbies for the downhills, pulling the handlebars to

---

AT A GLANCE

TRIP LENGTH 7 days

PHYSICAL CHALLENGE 1 2 3 ④ 5

MENTAL CHALLENGE 1 2 3 ④ 5

PRIME TIME Mid-March–early June; September–early November

PRICE RANGE (INDEPENDENT TRIP) $300

PRICE RANGE (OUTFITTED GROUP TRIP) $900

STAGING CITY Grand Junction, Colorado

HEADS UP Spring Break and October bring heavy crowds

Cranking up the slickrock, La Sal Mountains and Moab in the distance.

the chest for the uphills—kick their riding to a higher echelon. No longer do they walk the unthinkable. Moab, where the scenery often draws comparisons to Mars, is a strange, new world of mountain bike possibilities as well.

The sublime joys of sandstone are found on several Moab trails. Other rides involve limestone and gravel. But even on simple dirt roads, Moab riding is defined by rock: No other mtb destination, and few other deserts, bear witness to such stupendous flourishes of geology. In the 200 mil-

lion years that the Colorado Plateau has existed, wind and water have carved it into a maze of fantastic sculptures. Pillars, pedestals, windows, mesas, cliffs, and arches: The backdrops we saw on the "Coyote and Roadrunner Show" were not an exaggeration.

Moab has long profited from its landscapes: The nearby national parks, Arches and Canyonlands, have drawn tourists since the 1920s. Back then, Moab still retained vestiges of its founding. In 1855, Mormons established the Elk Mountain

Opposite: Getting away from Moab's mtb crowds, Canyonlands National Park.
Overleaf: The Navajo sandstone surface is smooth, but not slick; "mtb tires cling to it like cheese to pizza . . . "

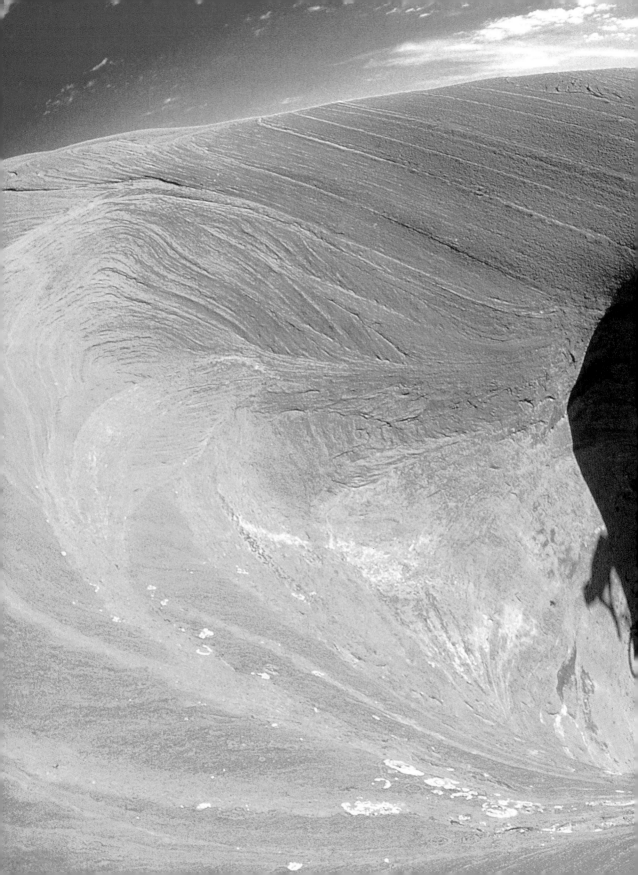

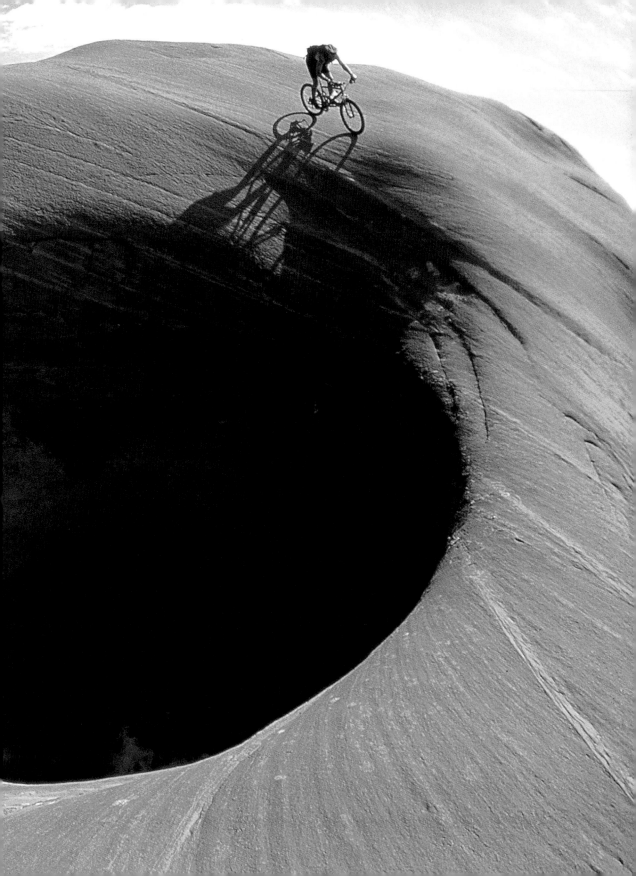

Riding on white rock, late afternoon, near Canyonlands National Park.

Mission to teach the Word to Ute Indians. The Utes tired of the humiliation in less than a year; they attacked and killed several Mormons, causing the survivors to abandon the mission. White ranchers and homesteaders kept trickling in, however. In 1881, they named the area Moab after an obscure town in the Bible. Except for a brief uranium boom in the 1950s, Moab remained a small town until the 1980s. Its claim to fame was hosting Hollywood filmmakers: Cheesy science fiction movies and old Westerns like *Wagonmaster* were shot here, as well as *Thelma and Louise* and *Mission Impossible 2*. Downtown Moab, in fact, is the site of the Hollywood Stuntmen's Hall of Fame, which houses lots of memorabilia from the Technicolor heyday of Westerns.

Mountain biking changed everything. Just when the sport began to boom—when thousands of newly minted riders were simultaneously wondering where to road trip—the mountain bike press started raving about Moab, and the Slickrock phenomenon. By the mid-1990s, more than 5,000 people lived in Moab, and tourists were bumping the peak-season population to 15,000. Motels sprouted on every corner. McDonald's led a stampede of nationally known franchises to Moab. The radio station began playing secular music.

Crowds have became a fact of life here. Lines sometimes form behind the technical hazards on the Slickrock Trail. Trailhead parking lots overflow on weekends. Yet on most trails, the crowds aren't too bothersome. For one, the great

Mesa Arch, Canyonlands National Park near Moab.

number of difficult rides in Moab thins the helmeted herd. Finding privacy isn't so hard—just veer over to the nearest cliffside aerie. During those stretches where you can't help but rub shoulders with fellow riders, ask them what kind of tires they like for sandstone. The argument that Moab's mass popularity ruins the quality of its biking? It doesn't wash.

I've ridden Moab often, yet every time I go, I still feel an urge to walk bowlegged and sing "Don't Fence Me In." I think Moab's mystique will endure so long as it remains our mind's-eye view of the big, open American West. Certainly no other mtb locale feels as downright grand as Grand County, Utah. In woodsy forests, a rider's perspective may not extend much wider than his handlebars. Moab, on the other hand, offers its horizons in huge, IMAX-like bursts.

Due to rocky ledges and other technical terrain, mountain biking in Moab makes you a better rider. It also makes you a scenery-gawking tourist who can burn through a couple of disposable cameras a day. Whether the resulting snapshots are in focus, your memories of riding the Mecca at the Center of the Universe will always be clear.

WHAT TO EXPECT

Moab is located in southeast Utah, 245 miles from Salt Lake City. The easiest way to get to Moab is via Interstate 70, 33 miles to the north. Moab's tiny airport serves only short shuttle flights from Salt Lake City. From Grand Junction, Colorado,

the nearest city with a full-service airport, it takes about two hours to drive to Moab.

Expect to see mountain biking in a brand-new light. If you've spent your mountain bike lifetime riding dirt, sandstone can seem odd at first. But after a few days in Moab, you'll quit seeing rocks as obstacles. Instead, you'll see where on the boulder you need to thread your front wheel.

A couple more things about rock: It is not pleasant to fall on. Wear a helmet and ride in control, and you can keep damage to a minimum. Also, Moab has many rides studded with small ledges. These can be jarring on the bike and the body. Anyone with a bad back should consider a full-suspension bike.

The only complaint most riders have with Moab is its shortage of singletrack. Porcupine Rim and Portal Trail are nice and narrow, but most rides involve dirt roads, jeep tracks and sandstone. The wider dirt roads can be boring, especially with a headwind, but the rest of Moab is challenging and entertaining enough that riders don't miss traditional singletrack.

The Moab Desert demands its own etiquette. Don't ride or walk over the cryptogamic soil. Made up of a combination of lichen, fungus, moss, and bacteria, this living organism literally holds the desert in place by slowing the erosion of soil due to wind and rain.

Watch where you're going. It's easy to lose the trail in the desert. There are usually cairns or painted marks to show you the way, but riders often miss them. Indeed, the Grand County Search and Rescue team often performs more than 100 rescues a year. In 1995, two Iowans

veered off trail, got stuck in a slickrock bowl, and died of exposure.

Moab's peak seasons are spring and fall. Winter brings chilly winds and summer sees temperatures in the 100s. Riding during peak season means crowds; avoid them by riding early or late in the day. At 4,000 feet elevation, Moab is the high desert. Still, heat exhaustion is a prominent danger here. Drink lots of water, and use your sunscreen.

For general information, contact the Grand County Travel Council (801-259-8825 or 800-635-MOAB) or the Utah Travel Council (801-538-1030 or www.netpub.com/utah!).

LODGING

The Mayor's House Bed & Breakfast (435-259-3019; 888-791-2345; email: rosetreeln@lasal.net) is decorated with earth tones reminiscent of Moab's southwestern setting. Amenities include swimming pool, hot tub, VCRs, and a grill. The Red Rock Lodge (435-259-5431; email: redrocklodge@lasal.net), an older motel located in a pleasant part of town, is clean and affordable.

There are nice campsites along the Colorado River and off Sand Flats Road near Slickrock Trail. Contact the Bureau of Land Management-Moab District (801-259-6111).

THE RIDES

The Slickrock Trail, located just above town off Sand Flats road, represents the essence of Moab. Every mountain biker needs to put this trophy on his mental shelf of great rides. Consisting of nearly 100 percent sandstone, Slickrock is

Opposite: The 12-mile Slickrock Trail, essence of the Moab mtb world, was originally founded by off-road motorcyclists. Above: Striped sandstone draws the eye—and the cyclist—inexorably forward.

It is possible, in slickrock country, to find yourself in some very tight places.

uniquely geologic even for Moab. Follow the little white lines dotting the rusty red rock. You'll be amazed at the pitches they climb, then further amazed that you can actually ride them. And the views of the Colorado River are a beautiful bonus. The 12-mile Slickrock Trail is a must.

Porcupine Rim Trail is a rollicking downhill, plus a fine avenue for viewing desert vistas. From the trailhead at the top of Sand Flats Road, you ride 4 miles up a gentle grade, then plunge 11 miles down to the Colorado. Rock formations

made famous in movies and Marlboro ads erupt from the valleys—Coffee Pot Rock on your left, Castle Rock and Priest & Nun on your right.

Moab Rim Trail is a steep, 7-mile pitch of rocky steps, slickrock slabs, and sand. Enjoy technical climbing to the top, home to the best birds-eye views of town. Then enjoy a quintessentially Moab downhill. It starts off narrow, flat, and fast, climbs through a sandy region, becomes rocky and steep as it descends, and eventually dissolves into a very scenic and challenging jeep road.

The sandy stretches at the beginning of Poison Spider Mesa are bothersome. Get past them and enjoy views of the Back of Behind fins set against the La Sal Mountains. Ride slickrock steeps to the top, then descend the cliff-clinging Portal Trail. Be careful: It's a highly technical singletrack all the way down, and a few riders have plunged to their deaths off the 400-foot drops.

OUTFITTERS AND BIKE SHOPS

Western Spirit, which conducts tours all over the country, is based in Moab and offers several local programs. The Moab Cyclery staff can point you to some of the best rides in Moab. Just go to Moab Cyclery in the middle of town next to the City Market. Another fine shop is Poison Spider Bicycles on Main.

MOAB CYCLERY
391 S. Main St.
Moab, UT 84532
435-259-7423

POISON SPIDER BICYCLES
497 N. Main St.
Moab, UT 84532
801-259-7882

WESTERN SPIRIT CYCLING
478 Mill Creek Dr.
Moab, UT 84532
800-845-2453, 435-259-8732
www.westernspirit.com
$595 for 4 days

RECOMMENDED READING

■ The *TRAILS ILLUSTRATED: MOAB AREA MOUNTAIN BIKE ROUTES* map, sold at several shops, is quite good.

■ *MOUNTAIN BIKING MOAB,* David Crowell (1997. $10.95. Falcon.) A clear, concise guidebook.

■ Bicycle Utah also publishes a free guide to biking the state: 801-649-5806.

■ *DESERT SOLITAIRE,* Edward Abbey (1991. $6.95. Ballantine Books.) A lyrical account of Abbey's three seasons as a park ranger in the Canyonlands. *Desert Solitaire* probably gets read in the campsites off Sand Flats Road more than any other book.

NOT SO SLICK

There's no slickrock on the Slickrock Trail. The Navajo sandstone-surfaced trail is called Slickrock due to a decision by the trail's builders. Incidentally, Slickrock was founded not by mountain bikers but by off-road motorcyclists. In 1969, the motos won permission from the Bureau of Land Management to build a trails route in the rocky outcrops east of Moab. They called it Bald Rock Bike Trail, but the name didn't stick. Neither did Bare Rock, Hard Rock, or Smooth Rock. They finally settled on the (current, world-renowned) name for the sound of it, even though "slickrock" technically refers to a much smoother type of sandstone.

Perhaps motorcyclists are geology purists who don't wish to sanction a Slickrock without slickrock: The trail's intended riders have never numbered more than 500 user days per year. Mountain bikers, meanwhile, lay rubber to Navajo sandstone constantly, racking up more than 100,000 user days per year.

Banff

How gorgeous are the Canadian Rockies? Magazines that run photographs of Banff-area lakes have been accused of airbrushing in that luminous blue.

Rich White is a mountain bike club leader in Southern California. He has sold mountain bikes, worked for component companies, led mtb tours, written for bike magazines, modeled for catalogs, raced in the expert class, and pretty much devoted his life to the sport. Rich has ridden all over America and many places abroad, and he lives in mtb-crazed Big Bear, California. So when Rich offers to share his ultimate mtb destination, you lean close and listen.

"Banff," he says.

"OK, dude, you can clear your throat first, and then tell me."

"No, I am telling you: You gotta ride Banff. As in Alberta's Banff National Park. Banff, along with surrounding areas like Canmore and Kananaskis, rules. It's one of those places where everywhere you look is stunningly beautiful."

Indeed it is. Situated in the Canadian Rockies

Valley of Ten Peaks at Moraine Lake near Lake Louise, Alberta, Canadian Rockies.

ALBERTA

Banff National Park

Calgary

Banff • • Canmore

Continental Divide

BRITISH COLUMBIA

Rocky Mountains

UNITED STATES

that loom majestically above Alberta's golden prairies, Banff was a no-brainer pick as Canada's first (and only the world's third) national park back in 1885. As Lynn Martel wrote a few years ago in *Bike* magazine, "The hanging glaciers, jagged rocky peaks, and jewel tone lakes put a kink in even a local's neck." Nonlocals, meanwhile, call it sacred. Banff is one of a few dozen Edens to merit inclusion on the World Heritage List, a roster of the globe's most unique and precious places compiled by the United Nations' World Heritage Convention.

Unlike most American national parks, where trail riding is rarely allowed, Banff offers hundreds of miles of singletrack. The surrounding areas add hundreds more. Rich likes to pedal them in summer, when the sun doesn't set till after 10. "I did double rides every day," says this sinewy greyhound who rides centuries almost weekly, "and I never saw the end to any trail or did the same one twice."

Rich and mountain bikers smart enough to emulate him ride fast and true through subalpine meadows, over pine-studded ridges, past steaming hot springs, and beneath rocky tusks such as the dramatic Mount Assiniboine. The singular joy of biking Banff, though, is skirting its gorgeous lakes, which are colored such a brilliant shade of blue that you'll flash back either to artistic depictions of Utopia or Tidy Bowl commercials. Magazines that run photographs of Banff-area lakes have occasionally been accused of airbrushing in that luminous blue. But such magazines are guilty only of glorifying rock flour—superfine grains of powder that have been ground up by the intense pressures of a glacier slowly scraping its way through the mountains. Escorted to the lakes by melting snow and ice, and suspended uniformly throughout the water, the rock flour particles are tiny and everywhere. They reflect lots of blue because, as colors go, blue has a tiny wavelength. Rock flour also keeps the lakes still and placid: Ripples are small and they dissipate quickly.

Then there's the wildlife. Banff is to North America what Kenya is to Africa, a region of insurmountable beauty that happens to contain a wealth of iconic animal species. Wolverines scrap in the woods while beavers and muskrats dip into the waters. An eagle migration route sends hundreds of birds of prey flying overhead. Most of the camcorder attention goes to what biologists call "charismatic megafauna," the large mammals padding about Banff's trails. Elk actually stroll down the streets of Banff, perhaps to escape the

AT A GLANCE

TRIP LENGTH 7 days
PHYSICAL CHALLENGE 1 2 3 ④ 5
MENTAL CHALLENGE 1 ② 3 4 5
PRIME TIME May–September

PRICE RANGE (INDEPENDENT TRIP) $280
PRICE RANGE (OUTFITTED GROUP TRIP) $1,200
STAGING CITY Calgary, Alberta
HEADS UP Bears are a legitimate threat—don't get between sows and cubs

packs of wolves. Meanwhile, moose and bighorn sheep bang antlers in the backcountry. Bears periodically maul clueless tourists. So many ursine brutes roam the woods that mountain bikers are advised to shout loudly and often. Says Rich, "Don't even think about riding Kananaskis without a 'bear bell.' These are regular bike bells, mind you, but locals call them bear bells because they have a higher purpose than *cling-cling* noises. Around Banff, they're used to save bikers' lives."

Bears have been dealing with permanent human clusters since 1883. It was then, two years before the driving of the last spike marked the completion of Canada's first transcontinental railroad, that three workers stumbled upon a series of hot springs on the lower shoulder of what is now called Sulphur Mountain. Back then, the train stop at the confluence of the Bow and Spray Rivers was called Siding 29 (further proof that railways shouldn't name romantic places). In 1885, though, Lord Mount Stephen rechristened it Banff because it reminded him of his home in Banffshire, Scotland.

After a heated ownership dispute, the spring and surrounding area were set aside and protected as a national park. The Canadian Pacific Railway immediately recognized the tourism potential of the Canadian Rockies and helped build the elegant 250-room Banff Springs Hotel. This structure's grand design and awesome alpine setting have made it as famous as Bavaria's Neuschwanstein. The railway then constructed a series of grand hotels along its main line and began advertising Banff as an international tourism stopover on the steel highway that was suddenly the fastest and most direct route from Europe to the Far East. The Canadian Rockies quickly became popular with the Victorian gentry, who came in droves to drink in the scenery and soak in the soothing hot springs.

In the ensuing decades, Banff has come to symbolize Canada's pristine beauty. Canadians are fiercely and justifiably proud of it—in part, perhaps, because even the swollen, egocentric superpower to the south can't match it. The 1988 Calgary Olympics, which staged many events in Banff, were especially glorious for those born under the Maple Leaf. And the Olympics alerted a new generation of recreationalists to the area's bounties. Indeed, the cross-country skiing venue of the '88 Games—the Cranmore Nordic Centre—was quickly morphed into a summer mtb hotspot.

These days, visitors to Banff see fewer Victorian ascots and more mountain biker bandanas. Of the 4 million people who visit Banff every year, many belong to the Clan of the Adventure Junkie. They snowboard in the winter, they rip singletracks in the summer, and, during the spring melt that prohibits snow and dirt endeavors, they go "ice-bergin'"—riding chunks of ice down the Bow River. It's gotten to the point that Banff's postal code—T0L 0C0—is inevitably pronounced as "too loco."

Opposite: The lakes of the Canadian Rockies are unrivaled for their beauty. Top: Riding along the Bow River, Banff Springs Hotel in the background. Above: Grizzlies are a real threat; avoid sows with cubs.

A singletrack trail near Tunnel Mountain Road in Banff, Bow River below.

don't mean PowerBars, but rather, biscuits and tea. A bloody nice way to prep for the ensuing 16-mile downhill, yes?

WHAT TO EXPECT

Banff is located in southwest Alberta, about 80 miles west of Calgary. American road-trippers might note that Banff sits about 120 miles from the United States border, almost due north above the intersection of Idaho and Montana. Banff's base elevation is 4,538 feet with nearby peaks stretching to 11,000 feet. The park itself is 2,654 square miles, but is surrounded by untold acres of undeveloped land: Of this, the prime mountain biking is found near Canmore and Kananaskis.

On both sides of the border, the Rockies are a challenging range. Although the British Columbia side receives more precipitation, Banff riders still deal with the extremes of mountain weather. Rides that commence with T-shirts can suddenly evolve into Gore-Tex-required slogs— or, failing a good jacket, teeth-chattering misery. Be ready for anything.

For information, contact the Alberta Visitors Bureau (800-661-8888) or Banff/Lake Louise Tourism Bureau (403-762-8421; www.banfflakelouise.com). For park specifics, call Banff National Park at 403-522-3833.

LODGING

Few hotels in the world can rival the majesty, hospitality, and scenery of the historic Banff Springs Hotel (800-441-1414; www.cphotels.com). For more than a century, this immense (250 rooms), opulent, castle-like hotel has towered above Banff, proving that, sometimes, manmade beauty can almost match nature's. No doubt you've seen pictures of the Banff Springs; if you can afford to splurge, stay there.

For elegance without so much grandeur, check out the Bed & Breakfast on Mountain Lane (403-762-2009; info@standish-banff.com)—a

Still, this New World playground retains a fair amount of Old World charm. As a quintessential chunk of Canada, it tempers its American-like rowdiness with dollops of British civility. Rich notes that Banff is "immaculate and the people actually act like they want you there. They're nice and they never get in your face." You'll understand when you moto your hardcore, USA-made dual-suspension rig to the lakeside Assiniboine Lodge—where post-ride afternoons

If you've got to "dismount" this clumsily, why not do so in heart-stoppingly stunning surroundings.

lodge that prides itself on its self-serve continental breakfast (you devour bagels, English muffins, scones, jams, cereals, fresh fruit, yogurt, juice, and coffee in your own suite) and its "Canadiana country décor."

If you're on a budget, make a base camp at either Buffalo Mountain Lodge (403-762-2400) or Brewster's Mountain Lodge (403-762-2900). Or try camping in the park; call 403-522-3833 for info.

THE RIDES

The trails are superb, lined with "tacky, grippy soil that loves knobbies." Because the Rockies that delineate the Alberta–British Columbia border just west of Banff soar above 11,000 feet, they intercept many eastbound storms. The clouds consequently dump most of their water in B.C., leaving the Alberta side relatively sunny and dry. The trails, then, take after the hard-packed wonders of Sun Valley, Idaho, and Bozeman, Montana. Smooth, solid dirt abounds—often framed by beatific stands of Douglas fir and aspen. Not that the riding is uniformly easy. The altitude alone can make the Canadian Rockies a wheeze-inducing test for lowland riders. And a landscape diverse enough to be a World Heritage site contains appropriate varieties of big rock, sidehill scree, and snaking roots.

The Lake Minnewanka ride remains the best

way to experience Banff's postcard terrain. Located a few miles northeast of Banff, its shoreline trail links forests of spruce to exposed alpine scree via 20 miles of roller-coaster singletrack. All the while you gape at icy, aqua-blue waters.

Another, slightly shorter classic is Jumping Pound/Cox Hill, located 12 miles south of Hwy. 68. Its 12 miles of singletrack involve wildflower-rich meadows, rocky staircases, big mountain views, and winding, technical descents.

Looking for an epic? Near Kananaskis Village, a great 40-plus-mile loop can be formed by combining four trails. Starting from the Barrier Dam, follow the Stoney Trail towards Kananaskis Village. Pick up the Skogan Pass Trail and follow it six miles over to Dead Man's Flats. Before reaching the highway crossing, turn right onto the Transcanada Trail into the Heart Creek trailhead parking area. Follow the Heart Creek Trail east to a gravel road and then turn right heading south. Climb over Jewel Pass and then descend back down to Barrier Lake.

The Canmore Nordic Centre in Canmore weaves miles of singletrack and fire roads in a dense crochet of fun mtb routes. Everyone from beginner to World Cup elite will find trails to his liking. The forested singletracks are commonly used in the Canada Cup race series; they boast several scary chutes and rooty drop-offs. Especially recommended are the Georgetown and Goat Creek trails. Finally, the facilities at the base include good food and free showers.

OUTFITTERS AND BIKE SHOPS

For intermediates and advanced riders, TrailMasters Mountain Bike Guides conducts all kinds of tours, including multi-day excursions into the backcountry. Unlimited Snowboards &

THE MOUNTIES

The Royal Canadian Mounted Police (RCMP), whose straight-backed "Mounties" represent perhaps Canada's most enduring national symbol, first made news in Alberta in 1873. The force had been assembled after the Canadian government decided to establish law and order on the frontier before allowing settlement so that Canada could avoid the experience of the United States, where the Western frontier was the scene of bloody warfare between indigenous peoples and white settlers. The Mounties' first job was to put down an illegal whiskey trading operation run by Montanans. Lightly armed, using horses for mobility, and clad in striking scarlet tunics, the Mounties marched into southern Alberta.

No matter how thoroughly you pedal Banff, rest assured that the Mounties rode harder and accomplished more. During Canada's formative years, they've tackled everything. Mounties brought deco-rum to the Klondike Gold Rush. They established a floating post in the Arctic islands and carried out pioneering dogsled expeditions across the eastern Arctic. The RCMP was in the forefront of counterespionage and countersubversion activity against the Cold War threat of Communism.

Today, the hardest-working national symbols extant fight Canada's battle against terrorism. Once an all-male force, the Mounties began recruiting women as peace officers in 1974. The force has also encouraged diversity by adapting its regulations to the needs of different cultural groups. An example is a recent decision allowing officers who are of the Sikh religion to wear turbans, as their religion requires, in place of the regulation Mountie hat. Horses, meanwhile, are getting squeezed out: The modern Mountie travels by airplane, automobile, boat, snowmobile, power toboggan, and, yes, mountain bike.

Mountain Bikes provides good bike service in downtown Banff.

TRAILMASTERS MOUNTAIN BIKE GUIDES LTD.
P.O. Box 8052
Canmore, Alberta, T1W 2T8, Canada
403-678-0384
www.canadianrockies.net/trailmasters
$800 for 5 days

UNLIMITED SNOWBOARDS & MOUNTAIN BIKES
111 Banff Avenue
Banff, Alberta, T0L 0C0, Canada
403-762-3725

RECOMMENDED READING

■ *HANDBOOK OF THE CANADIAN ROCKIES*, Ben Gadd (1996. $35.95. Corax Press.) A nice general guidebook.

■ Riders should look up the detailed mtb guidebook, *BACKCOUNTRY BIKING IN THE ROCKIES* (403-249-9490), and *GEM TREK RECREATION MAPS* (403-932-4893), especially map numbers 5, 6, 7, and 8.

■ *BACKCOUNTRY BIKING IN THE CANADIAN ROCKIES*, Doug Eastcott (1999. $16.95. Rocky Mountain Books.)

■ *LEANING ON THE WIND: UNDER THE SPELL OF THE GREAT CHINOOK*, Sid Marty (1998. $19.00. Harper Collins Canada.) Aptly honors Alberta's unique blend of prairie and mountains. Winner of a 1995 Banff Mountain Book Festival Award, *Leaning on the Wind* explores Canada's wild (and not-so-wild) West with piercing observations and wry humor.

Valley of the Ten Peaks. Unlike most U.S. national parks, which prohibit singletrack biking, Banff offers hundreds of miles of trails.

Vancouver

In the technical skills capital of the sport, the trails are like lightning strikes from an angry god—intense revelation accompanied by a robust spank.

In my first two days riding within Vancouver's orbit, I pedaled the most technical, whacked-out terrain imaginable. You need ride here only a little to understand why local trail builders give their creations such graphic names. They sound like threats: The Dentist; Shit Happens; Blood, Sweat, & Fear; Tracks from Hell; The Crippler; Nine Lives; The Reaper; Thrill Me, Kill Me; Meet Yer Maker; and Severed Dick. It's S&M mountain biking at its finest. Thank you, sir, may I have another?

The trails were like lightning strikes from an angry god—intense revelation followed by a robust spank. I'd never ridden anything like them anywhere. Living in California at the time, my idea of a good ride entailed long climbs, hard packed soil, cleanable obstacles, and open views. On my home turf, I felt more than competent.

But riding the River Runs Through It trail, on a dripping, numb-finger day during the annual

Catching air on My Friend the Grouse Trail, Cypress Mountain, North Shore Vancouver, overlooking downtown Vancouver.

BRITISH COLUMBIA

Coast Mountains

Vancouver Island

PACIFIC

Whistler

Grouse Mtn

Vancouver

Victoria

Seattle

WASHINGTON

October monsoon, I bumbled and tumbled till I almost crumbled. Every big-log drop-off, of which there were dozens, commissioned a visit to nose wheelie city. My rear tire wasn't just slipping off roots; it was pulling the "electric slide" à la James Brown. The darkest moment came when rounding a turn to find that the trail crossed a 40-foot-wide river via a log positioned six feet above the water. A few two-by-six planks had been affixed to the top of the log, however—making it rideable, though still sketchy for anyone lacking a Cirque du Soleil sense of balance. I got maybe a quarter of the way across it before my bruised confidence took over and yanked hard on the brakes. This brilliant move, of course, pitched my rear tire sideways with great violence. Only the quick, heroic intervention of two Velociraptor tire lugs saved me from a raging case of hypothermia.

I walked across as a humbled (but suddenly enlightened) man. All my problems, I realized, owed to braking. In my earnestness to respect the terrain's wild undulations, I was overdosing on lever pulling. It goes against basic human instincts to fly full tilt at slimy two-foot-high log barriers, but that's exactly what Vancouver's legion of elite mountain bikers do. Speed carries you right over your assorted hindrances. Hesitation, on the other hand, gets you nowhere.

This is especially true in the dark, primeval forests of the "super, natural" province. Braking here may seem like a good idea, but it ends up becoming a more or less futile attempt to impose your will on a land that just won't have it. In southwest B.C., you don't control the trail. The trail controls you.

The North Shore of Vancouver, in particular, is mountain biking's radical frontier. Separated from the rest of the city by an inlet, the North Shore is its own distinct region. Essentially, it's 100,000 or so people wedged between the inlet and three big, steep peaks: Cypress, Grouse, and Seymour. These days, the Shore is changing mountain biking as we know it. Vancouver shapes bike imagery—mags, ads, and, especially, videos. It's led to all kinds of product innovations, such as stem-pads and riser bars. The people who ride it include bent math teachers like "Dangerous Dan" Cowan, the Olympic medalist Alison Sydor, and X Games stars like Andrew Shandro. Many belong to a phenomenon created on the North Shore: sponsored teams of "freeriders." They don't race;

AT A GLANCE

TRIP LENGTH 7 days	PRICE RANGE (INDEPENDENT TRIP) $300
PHYSICAL CHALLENGE 1 2 3 4 ⑤	PRICE RANGE (OUTFITTED GROUP TRIP)
MENTAL CHALLENGE 1 2 3 ④ 5	$600–$1,000
PRIME TIME April–September	STAGING CITY Vancouver, British Columbia
	HEADS UP Bring new, grippy tires for slick roots and mud

Riding The Reaper, Cypress Mountain, North Shore.

they get paid because they can ride anything and look good for the camera.

Many trails on the North Shore are impossible to ride up. Instead you ride paved roads up, then enter the woods for sick descents. You've heard of "trials" riding, the flashy, stunt-happy arm of mountain biking in which hypercoordinated riders hop on their tires from, say, the stage onto David Letterman's desk? Well, Vancouver's descents are commonly described as "downhill trials."

And the paths that descend the Shore's slick, mossy slopes are not sanctioned by any park or government agency. They're much too steep and hazard prone. No, these trails are the privately built, quasi-legal creations of characters like "Dangerous Dan" Cowan and Gabe "Goat Legs" Szczurek. They simply explored tangles of hemlock, maple, fir, and cedar and found old skidder roads (down which the logging companies once dragged trees). They rode and hacked these till a defined trail emerged, then marked them with scary omens like a broken bike helmet or a hangman's noose. Cowan says the idea wasn't so much to provide recreational opportunities for the active lifestyle market, but rather, to link series of

Opposite: A Douglas fir across the trail creates a perfect big-log drop-off, another of the many thrilling challenges of Vancouver riding.

"cunning stunts." For instance, the immense cedar log suspended 10 feet over a ravine. You ride along it till the point of no return, then you must ride up and over a plywood teeter totter—all for the privilege of continuing along the log!

Along with the stunts are technical nightmares such as the one on Ladies Only trail called The Big Stupid. According to writer Mitchell Scott, "It's a 16-feet-high, 65 degree tire-scraped chunk of granite that hurls you between two clavicle-cracking cedars." In local parlance, this kind of a drop is a "slider": an absurdly steep pitch where you accelerate even when both brakes are locked up.

To ride the steeps of the Shore, you must scoot so far back over the rear tire that you risk the "rubber enema." Even the locals crash constantly. If they're lucky, they catapult past the boulders and python-sized root systems and instead land on the rotting logs or mulchy loam.

Receiving 91 inches of precipitation per year, the Shore is a sopping Middle Earth of green growth. How thick is it? A large jet crashed into the North Shore in 1947. It wasn't found until 1994.

The copious rain may remind some of a certain island kingdom, but somewhere along the line, Vancouver phased the "British" out of British Columbia. I reckon there's more Anglo-priggishness in Peter Jennings' sneering upper lip than the whole of southwest B.C. Both a haven for 1960s draft dodgers and the buckle of the province's infamous cannabis belt, Vancouver is the undisputed locus of Canada's counterculture. Throw in the mild weather and stunning beauty of the Coast Range, and it's no wonder that Vancouver attracts recreation junkies by the VW vanful. The result: lots of fit, young people who act as straight as cooked spaghetti and are just as likely to shout "Semper Fi." Mountain bikers—who are naturally fond of inhaling free spirit—ride amok here. Since the early 1980s, Vancouver has served as the sport's renegade hotbed. An early race called Black Hole required riders to pedal up a huge sewer, past tumbling rocks, and into a lake where they'd have to tag a rubber chicken.

A sense of humor comes in handy here, where the trails routinely demand that you perform some sort of slapstick. But stick it out, and eventually you'll feel reverence for this mountain-ringed coastal inlet. There will come a moment when the rigors of biking Vancouver will provide you with the skill to handle it. For me, that moment came at Alice Lake Provincial Park. On a network of trails used for a venerable B.C. mtb race called Test of Metal, my partners and I whipped through turns and humped over roots and rocks under the graceful canopy of 100-foot-tall cedar trees. We did this while staying on the bikes instead of watching them cartwheel off into the woods. There's no better feeling than smoking a switchback that drops six feet and is tighter than

THE DARK SIDE OF THE PACIFIC RIM

Vancouver feels like a Canadian hybrid of Seattle–San Francisco–Los Angeles, more West Coast than Great White North. And it maintains such strong ties to Asia that a term as artificial sounding as "capital of the Pacific Rim" rings true here. The flip side, which would be sad if it weren't so weird, is that almost 25 percent of the city's murder victims buy it in karaoke bars. No lie: In 1996, the karaoke gangster movement accounted for five of Vancouver's (preposterously low) 22 homicides. Authorities are now warning anyone who feels an overwhelming urge to sing "Seasons in the Sun" to just do it in the shower.

a game of Twister in a phone booth. When we paused to take a break and sit on some big trees, a rainbow suddenly arced across the Cheekye River. The only thing missing was the orchestra.

Alice Lake, like just about every place we rode in or near Vancouver, was tight and twisty and fun. The cliché is that trails like this make you drool. The reality is the opposite: Vancouver trails are so intense, they leave you cotton-mouthed. Senses are jolted alive and stretched thin. There's never, ever any time to relax on the saddle, because the second you do, a root as thick as a telephone pole tries to knock your fork up through your arms and into your teeth. You need rest stops to help your eyeballs relax. An end result is that a two-hour ride here enervates you as much as a five-hour ride at home.

Unlike anything at home, riding Vancouver induces a mental and physical transformation. You ride stuff you previously considered unridable. That's the beauty of doing hellaciously technical trails. Eventually, your fearful avoidance of obstacles becomes a willful acceptance. The trail's not getting any easier, so you get better. Go to southwest B.C. and you'll return with new skills and aptitudes. It's as dependable as rain in monsoon season, as sure as moss in an old-growth forest.

WHAT TO EXPECT

Vancouver, Canada's principal Pacific seaport, sits at the mouth of the Burrard Inlet in the southwestern corner of the huge province of British Columbia. While there are great mtb trail systems from the coast all the way to the Alberta border, nothing else quite lives up to the mystique surrounding Vancouver. Riders who enjoy challenge should also ride in Squamish and the resort town of Whistler (both are reached within 90 minutes by the gorgeous Sea to Sky Highway).

While there are many options for less psychotic riders, Vancouver deserves its reputation as the globe's most challenging mountain bike destination. A common surface is "corduroy"—a series

Catching air off a ramp, The Roach Hit, Cypress Mountain, North Shore Vancouver.

of wooden planks laid along the trail, leftovers from when logging companies would roll makeshift trains up with mill parts and such. Riding it requires you to throw your front wheel forward and try to match the rhythm of the planks: *lunka, chunk, lunka.*

Around here, a sloppily performing bike is downright dangerous. Make sure your brakes are tight; even if they are, it's a good idea to bring spare brake pads because the wet weather chews them quickly. To deal with the steepness of Vancouver trails, local riders use short stems and upsweeping handlebars. They lower their seat for the plunges, so quick-release seatposts are almost universal. Many ride with shin and forearm pads in anticipation of the inevitable dismounts.

The forest mulch is so accustomed to rain and so full of organic matter other than dirt, that the trails don't erode much. Thus, riding in wet

Another crafty creation of "Dangerous Dan" Cowan, Grouse Mountain, North Shore Vancouver.

weather isn't frowned on like it is in, say, Durango. Deal with the rain by bringing a top-level Gore-Tex jacket, warm tights, and full-fingered gloves. Waterproof socks, like the Sugoi models made in Vancouver, are recommended, too.

Late spring through September constitutes prime mtb season (though Whistler doesn't thaw till June). October can be magnificent, but as the start of monsoon season, it can also be drenching.

For general information, contact the North Vancouver Chamber of Commerce (604-987-4488; www.cofcnorthvan.org) or the British Columbia Ministry of Tourism (800-663-6000; www.tbc.gov.bc.ca/tourism/information.html).

LODGING

The Lynnwood Inn (604-988-6161; www.lynnwoodinn.com) stands out from the other B&Bs on the North Shore because it embraces the area's funky side, including mountain biking. A great little hotel, it contains a coffee shop and pub.

In Squamish, a new Super 8 Motel (604-815-0883) offers clean (if somewhat sterile) rooms near good riding.

THE RIDES

Ladies Only, located on Grouse Mountain, is one of the original and more famous North Shore trails. Some flat sections interrupt a good dose of steep, sometimes rooty, sometimes rocky drops.

Stunts include a log ride with a teeter-totter on it, several ramps over logs, and a few ladder bridges. One of the bigger attractions on the trail is the rock/cliff whose three parallel routes have been properly dubbed Semi-retarded, Big Stupid, and the Milky Way. The trail flows nicely and is great to practice on for the bigger stunts. Find it on the fifth switchback up from the bottom of the Grouse Mountain fire road.

Roach Hit is a fun, fast, consistently steep trail on Cypress Mountain. Like many North Shore trails, it's not marked; find it on the main Cypress road off the right side of the logging road coming down from the second viewpoint. Roach Hit contains several rock drops varying in size from two to six feet, plus a couple of very aesthetic jumps and bank turns.

Rollercoaster is located in Pacific Spirit Park near the University of British Columbia. Considered the sweetest, smoothest, fastest singletrack in Vancouver, it blends huge ups and downs with an insanely twisting path.

OUTFITTERS AND BIKE SHOPS

Singletrack Adventures combines tours of Vancouver and Whistler with gourmet food. Experts may prefer to hook up with North Shore MTB Tours, which makes no bones about taking hardcore riders to the area's "natural and man-made stunts."

The Deep Cove Bike Shop is home to wild riders, helpful mechanics, crazy trail builders, various other true believers, speakers pumping reggae, handmade bikeswith quasi-obscene names like Hummer and Handjob, and an indefinable mtb spirit/karma/attitude/funk/vibe.

SINGLETRACK ADVENTURES

3704 Hawthorne Ave.
Terrace, BC, V8G 5E2, Canada
888-711-5333
www.singletrackbc.com
$1,200 for 6 days

Winter wonderland on Grannies Trail, Mount Fromme.

NORTH SHORE MTB TOURS

6048 Gleneagles Dr.
West Vancouver, BC, V7W 1W2, Canada
604-861-7140
www.northshoretours.com
$90 per day

THE DEEP COVE BIKE SHOP

4310 Gallant Ave.
North Vancouver, BC, V7G 1K8, Canada
604-929-1918
www.covebike.com

RECOMMENDED READING

■ *MOUNTAIN BIKE! SOUTHWESTERN BRITISH COLUMBIA: A GUIDE TO THE CLASSIC TRAILS.* Ward Cameron (1999. $15.95. Menasha Ridge.)
■ *LEGENDS OF VANCOUVER,* E. Pauline Johnson-Tekahionwake (1998. $12.95. Douglas & McIntyre Ltd.) Written in 1911, it essentially describes Salish Indian mythology from an oral history given to the author by Chief Joe Capilano. Readers learn much about the Salish's fascinating customs and the rich cultural life of Canada's lower Pacific Coast.

Lago di Garda & the Dolomites

La dolce vita is raging among the velo-philes occupying these sun-kissed lakes and craggy peaks.

Literally speaking, "la dolce vita" is the Italian translation of "the sweet life." It's also a kind of cultural directive; a nationwide push to milk human existence for all it's worth.

When mountain biking the Dolomites and Lago di Garda, you witness a million different quests for happiness and beauty. Intricately painted flower boxes. Middle-aged women pulling their shirts down to better tan their chests. Roadside truck stops serving savory panini sandwiches on real dishes—not paper or plastic. A five-star restaurant, that boasts a wine cellar holding 30,000 bottles, staffed by waiters wearing decorative bow-ties of straw. If a rainy day keeps you inside, you notice that Italian television game shows are so resplendent with bright colors and sparkly baubles, they make "The Price Is Right" set look positively Luddite.

Plain things are embellished, empty spaces are adorned. In the States, jackets serve mainly to

Path through an olive grove near Lago di Garda. Northern Italy has welcomed all things mtb.

protect people from the weather. "BOR-ing!" say our Italian counterparts. To them, a jacket is a showcase for the wonders of gold lamé or purple paisley. An unseemly number of jackets bear words and phrases, which for some reason are always in English. Over the course of 12 days traveling in northern Italy, I saw some doozies. "Challenge the Wind!" advised one. An especially shiny piece informed viewers that "Reptiles are great. They're the toast of the town. Live's (sic) always better with reptiles around." I'm not making this up. Still another parka asked onlookers to "Beat the Wanderers." Inspired, I vowed to pummel any and all wanderers, to rip off their arms and beat them with their own severed limbs.

OK, so that's an exaggeration. But it's true that Italians strive to add color and excitement to a place that . . . well, doesn't need any embellishment at all.

The Dolomites run in a northeasterly direction across the pocket of northern Italy that's east of Switzerland and directly south of Innsbruck, Austria. Lago di Garda sits just south of the mountains.

Lago di Garda, a breathtaking mountain lake lined with noble forests, inspired poets and artists well before it attracted tourists. Its broad southern end resembles an inland sea. The north shore, meanwhile, evokes fjords, for the water is hemmed in by the craggy magnificence of the Dolomites, a sub-range of the Alps and one of the world's most distinct mountain ranges. Blessed with countless cathedrals of stratified rock—massifs, spires, buttes, notches, needles, slabs, and cones—the range makes Monument Valley look puny and empty. The entire area seems to bathe in golden light. Indeed, the climate on the Italian slope of the Alps is usually 10 degrees warmer than the nearby Austrian side. And it's almost unfair to compare the relative warmth of the people.

In Northern Italy, the European passion for road riding has translated freely to mountain biking. While skinny-tire snobbery seems to discourage trail access in France and Britain, Italian officials have opened the North to all things mtb. Every spring, Lago di Garda happily hosts the globe's largest mtb festival, attracting as many as 20,000 riders to its rocky dirt roads, twisty singletracks, and ancient cart

Overleaf: Riding the trails on Monte Tremalzo (5,400 feet) above Riva del Garda village at north end of the lake.

AT A GLANCE

TRIP LENGTH 8 days

PHYSICAL CHALLENGE 1 2 3 (4) 5

MENTAL CHALLENGE 1 2 (3) 4 5

PRIME TIME May–September

PRICE RANGE (INDEPENDENT TRIP) $700

PRICE RANGE (OUTFITTED GROUP TRIP) $1,300

STAGING CITY Milan, Italy

HEADS UP Some rides compel you to share roads with notorious Italian drivers

paths. The province of Trentino alone marks and maintains more than 2,900 miles of trails and roads that are off-limits to cars.

Declaring the region one of the "Most Beautiful Places on Earth" to ride, *Bike* magazine testified that "Centuries of hiking culture have interlaced the Dolomites with some of the world's most intricate, well-marked, and well-maintained trails. Topo maps are covered with mazes of squiggly red lines, each one labeled with a number that can be found on one of the regularly spaced signposts along the trail." They link alpine valleys, fast-flowing rivers, fields of wildflowers, and whitewashed towns dominated by church towers.

A typical ride may begin in a tidy town square, where you'll fill your bottles with the clear cold water issuing from a stone fountain. You'll struggle up a steep trail, perhaps encountering a group of hikers led by a priest. *"Forza e coraggio,"* he'll smile, ("Be strong and brave"). Channeling your *"Vis et Robur"* (the local, Latin term for "hope and strength"), you'll keep climbing into the woodland home of deer, white ptarmigan, and chamois. In the highest, remotest country you might see a religious pilgrim striding barefoot while wearing a coarse tunic. You'll descend ancient footpaths back down to civilization and the deservedly celebrated marvels of Northern Italian carbo loading.

It's little wonder that Lago di Garda has become mountain biking's hottest word-of-mouth travel tip. Italy's official tourist offices couldn't rave about it as effusively as the riders who've visited. Witness this random collection of reviews from an mtb website:

"These trails are among the best you will ever find on the planet."

"The Lago di Garda area is a mountain biker's paradise with rolling mountains surrounding a long lake."

"Some of the best trails I've ever been on."

"The days weren't long enough."

"If I could, I'd give the place ten stars. It's that good, really!!!"

From the lake (elevation: 750 feet), the mountains rise as high as 6,500 feet. There are several ride choices for each ability level. Monte Brione is the most popular, the peak that everyone raves about, and it sometimes gets too crowded for the rider seeking solitude. A roughly elliptic peak, Brione's west side sits nearly level with the lake while the east end slopes up and then drops sharply. It looks like a large cylinder buried at an angle. A road leads up and ends at a large bunker near the top. From there you drop down one of a variety of serpentine singletracks, the most technical of which is a World Cup course on the eastern edge. Brione has terrain for everyone, but is best known for short, often difficult rides.

Longer and still more challenging rides exist on the slopes of Monte Tremalzo, south of Riva del Garda village. Most of the trails on Monte Tremalzo reach an elevation of about 5,900 feet.

Top: Swans on Garda. Above: The mountains rise from the lake as high as 6,500 feet. Opposite: The village of Malcesine on the northeast shore of Lago di Garda, with Gruppo di Brenta (the Brenta peaks) of the Dolomites in the distance.

They make frequent small climbs and dips. To keep things interesting, many of the paths employ rock gardens and loose gravel.

Farther north, in the Dolomites, each pedal stroke seems to spin up a history lesson. The area's striking geology owes to the withdrawal of the Tethys Sea 250 million years ago. It was a

A sanctuary in Tignate, on the very steep northwest coast.

warm sea, rich with crustacea and coral. When the water disappeared, these living organisms fossilized and grew—ascending skyward faster than the process of erosion.

Valleys in the Dolomites have been settled—and seriously coveted—for a thousand years. Attila's Huns, Theodoric's Ostrogoths, the Longobards, the Franks, and the Bavarians all attacked the area in the first millennium after Christ, and often succeeded. Historians speculate that this very subjection to different regimes imbued the Dolomiti people with their spirit of independence. Even in the last century, Austrian and Italian interests have battled for control of the Dolomites; judging by the proliferation of German signs and speakers, neither has clearly won.

The territory skirmishes in World War I, in fact, led to the Dolomite's incredible array of roads and trails. In two and a half years of hellish trenchline battle, neither the Italians nor the Austrians gained much ground. But they sure tried—leaving behind all kinds of paths, tracks, dugouts, and turrets. Mountain bikers often stumble upon the soldiers' rusted tin cans, barbed wire, and bullet casings.

Compared to Lago di Garda, mountain biking in the Dolomites takes place at significantly higher altitudes (as high as 8,000 feet) and intersects with humanity much less often. The sheer faces and labyrinthine folds of the Dolomites can discourage the huge tour buses that ply the rest of the Alps, so mountain bikers can often ride for days without seeing another fat-tire pilot. When noodling from saddle to dramatic saddle, you can enjoy solitude. When rocketing down the Dolomites' huge escarpments (4,000 vertical feet), you can usually let off the brakes. Riding mostly above timberline, you gaze at horizons roiling with awesome sculpted rock. Of course, the Italians adorn even these: In craggy nooks where mountain goats fear to tread, they erect cozy *rifugios*, weathered wooden huts that serve steaming cappuccinos and offer rustic lodging for long-distance riders. The combination of Italian sunshine, hearty pastas, and sassy chiantis makes the *rifugios* notoriously hard to leave. In short, the Dolomites represent a nearly ideal range for cycling. It seems somehow fitting that, in the local lexicon, clusters of Dolomite peaks go by the same name as mtb component sets: *gruppos*.

After a memorable day playing in the Alta Badia section of the Dolomites, I sat down to dinnner with Christian, a new Italian friend. As we ate flavorful horsemeat carpaccio—a local Dolomiti delicacy—I asked him about the spires, massifs, and sheer rock faces that framed so many excellent rides. He gazed out at the rugged, frost-etched peaks thrusting thousands of feet above the gentle valleys. The waning sun, which had been bathing the western faces in ochre light, began to brush in some darker orange. "The Dolomites, they are like monuments," said Christian. "They are always beautiful, and in the evening, they become lovely with red and purple. I think they are very happy mountains."

WHAT TO EXPECT

You'll fly into Milan; from there it's about a three-hour drive to Lago di Garda.

Currently there are no restrictions to cycling on forest roads or singletracks. Still, ride with etiquette. Hiking, which remains a more popular way to explore the Northern Italian mountains, will occasionally deposit slow-footed, slow-witted beasts in your path. Pull over and greet them with a *"Buongiorno,"* and everyone will enjoy his day.

Forest roads are well maintained and normally pleasant to ride, with good gravel roadbed and reasonable steepness, rarely more than 10 percent. There are legions of sweet singletracks; beware that many contain wheeze-inducing steeps and rough surfaces. Because the rock is very sharp and edgy, pinch flats happen often here. Take at least two spare tubes on every ride.

Ambitious mountain bikers may want a car to reach distant trailheads, though trains routinely add cars for bike transport. Plus, bikes are allowed on some of the many cableways here: Arranging a sweat-free downhill ride is pretty simple.

On the roads around Lago di Garda, there are numerous small tunnels—dark ones. A taillight or an LED flasher is essential, as Italian drivers are not known for their careful slow speeds.

Lago di Garda's weather is usually kind. But in the Dolomites, clouds and mist can blow in quickly, obscuring trails. Summer travelers will need to plan around afternoon thunderstorms.

The number for the Italian Tourism Board in the United States is 212-245-4822. For more directed information contact the local outfits. Lago di Garda's main tourist office answers its local phone at 91-62-45. English speakers may prefer to surf to www.garda.com, which offers links to most conceivable Garda enterprises, including its mammoth mountain bike festival (usually held in early May). For the Dolomites, see www.dolomiti.it/eng/zone/cortina or www.sunrise.it/dolomiti. e-mail: apt1@sunrise.it).

ROCK OF AGES

The name "Dolomites" derives from the rock's first official scholar, the French geologist Deodat-Guy-Sylvain-Tancre de Gratet de Dolomieu (1750–1801), who in 1789 was so fascinated by the area's stratified carbonate rock that he sent samples to Switzerland for classification. These were returned with the announcement that their geological composition—hitherto unknown—warranted their naming after the "founder." (In truth, the rock had probably been found by 1789. The Frenchman's rock varies in appearance: some is more stratified and folded than others and contains thick layers of seaweed, coral and other organisms that lived in the ancient Tethys Sea.

LODGING

In Riva del Garda, stay at the Hotel Sole (39-55-26-86). This pretty but affordable hotel overlooks the lake, and was once philosopher Friedrich Nietzsche's favorite place to bunk.

L'Hotel Zanella (39-0464 50-51-54; www.mtb.ongarda.com/hotel; hotelzanella@ongarda.com), a three-star hotel located along Lago di Garda in the quiet town of Nago, offers a pool, a tennis court, a private beach, and bike storage.

Dolomite lodgers should make their way to Corvara and the Hotel Tablé, (39-0471 83-61-44; hotel.table@rolmail.net) a three-star hotel staffed with incredibly nice people.

Even if you don't stay there, take at least one night to splurge at the hotel/restaurant with the 30,000 bottle wine cellar, the outrageously good La Perla (39-0471 83-61-32; perla@altabadia.it) in Corvara. You may not know now that you crave pumpkin ravioli with truffle oil, but believe me, you do. The centuries-old hotel, incidentally, is a luxurious, eccentric structure with a waterfall-blessed spa and elegant wooden beams.

The Dolomites also boast a well-ordered system of 100-plus *rifugi*, or mountain huts, where you can wait out inclement weather and overnight in dorm-style bunk rooms for a nominal fee, usually about $10 (stop in any local tourist office for info).

THE RIDES
LAGO DI GARDA

The town of Riva del Garda is the prime base for biking the Lago di Garda region. Riva offers easy access to the sunny trails lacing the ridgeline above the lake. For a good challenge, try climbing 6,815-foot Monte Alltissimo.

The Santa Colomba Trail is a fine ride near the city of Trento. The trail climbs three thousand feet up Mount Calisio, moves clockwise around the peak, and continues on a small plateau on its northern side. It reaches the small Lake of Santa Colomba. From there you partly retrace your steps, complete a full turn around Calisio, and finish with an entertaining downhill ride back to town.

DOLOMITES

From Cortina, the best-known resort town in the Dolomites, ride the Val di Gotres. It's a nice 20-mile loop that combines all the Dolomite hallmarks: a healthy climb on World War I roads, alpine meadows, a charming rifugio (Ra Stua), a rocky downhill to a quaint village (San Uberto), and, finally, a singletrack through a gorge back to Cortina.

Atop Alpe di Siusi, near the town of Ortisei, you can ride a network of grainy hiking lanes, gravel farm roads, and dirt singletrack. Ascend a tram, pedal to the base of the massive spires of the Sassolungo gruppo, then coast downward for 10 miles and 4,000 vertical feet.

OUTFITTERS AND BIKE SHOPS

Too Fast-Trentino Bike is a local mtb institution: It offers a variety of multi-day tours, ranging from moderate to challenging.

In Riva del Garda, take your shop needs to Centro Cicli Pederzolli or Girelli.

Most of the ski shops in Dolomite villages also offer at least some mountain bike service in the summer.

TOO FAST-TRENTINO BIKE
39-0464 50-61-49
www.mtb.ongarda.com; toofast@anthesi.com

CENTRO CICLI PEDERZOLLI
Viale Canella
Riva del Garda, Italy
39-55-42-30

GIRELLI
Viale Damiano Chiesa 15/17
Riva del Garda, Italy
39-55-66-02

RECOMMENDED READING

■ *LONELY PLANET ITALY* (1996. $17.95. Lonely Planet.) Devotes a few useful chapters to the northern regions.

■ Dropping into local tourist office should net you lots of info on mtb trails, including maps. Some offices will have some small booklets issued by local mountain biking clubs, which are quite useful because of the local knowledge involved. Pick up a map from Kompass if you can (available at www.dolomiti.it/eng/zone/cortina): These are standard for Northern Italian adventurers, and the company recently introduced three mtb-specific guides for Lago di Garda.

■ *DOLOMITES: JOURNEY THROUGH AN ENCHANTED KINGDOM,* Cristina Todeschini Translated by Ivor Neil Coward. (1998. $25. Light Hunter Publications.) A photographic and descriptive portrait of Italy's most stunning range, *Dolomites* qualifies as a "coffee-table book." Maybe "espresso-table book" works better, for this is an energetic, heartily Italian refreshment. Dolomites blends pithy essays, trivia-laced sidebars, highly informative captions, vintage lithographs, and tack-sharp photographs dripping with color.

World-class mountain biker Hans Rey above Lago di Garda, final day of Rey's 8-day trans-Alp crossing, September 1999.

The West

Tarzan fans will love these thick, wildlife-filled jungles, where snaking through on a mountain bike seems only marginally inferior to swinging on vines.

After a few days of hiking in the chilly mists that cloak Costa Rica's Monteverde Cloud Forest, my partner and I headed south, and downhill, for warmer climes. We drove until the pines gave way to palms. Then we pulled out the bikes and set off down a random dirt road. We'd just hit a good spinning rhythm when we passed a little swatch peeling off to the right. We both hit the brakes and traded "did you see what I think I saw?" looks. It was a single-track, headed God knows where.

We pounced on it, dirt hissing and leaves crackling beneath our tires. The vegetation thickened dramatically about 300 yards from the trailhead. We were enveloped by towering green; overhanging branches linking together to screen out the sky. The blades of palm fronds scissored together with an audible *whttt*, an unseen bird cawed, and a butterfly fluttered by in a hallucination of red and black. I had

Costa Rica has protected 27 percent of its land, the highest percentage of any country on earth.

NICARAGUA

COSTA RICA
▲ Arenal Volcano
CARIBBEAN
Monteverde ⊙ San José
Puntarenas
Manuel
Antonio
PANAMA

PACIFIC   Osa Peninsula

dreamed of exploring the tropical jungle since I was 13, when I devoted a miserably hot summer to reading every single book in the *Tarzan* series, all 26 of them. Finally, I was in the thick of the jungle, and snaking through on a mountain bike seemed only marginally inferior to swinging on vines.

We penetrated further, the jungle closing in all the while. We didn't so much follow a trail as will one to happen. Finally, it stopped altogether. I looked for a clue as to why the path had come even this far—a mile maybe—and found it in the form of a discarded Pampers box. On the steep hillside above it, there stood a small grove of wild lemon trees. A harvester had apparently brought more boxes than he could fill.

We rode back out to the main road with a new appreciation for our mountain bikes and their unmatched ability to penetrate unknown environments. Our little detour to the lemon grove was by no means an adrenaline-fueled thrill ride. Rather, it was an exploration, one that benefited our minds as much as our lungs. You can say the same about many of this nation's rides. Not that Costa Rica lacks for physical thrills. But even the roller coaster rides seem humbled by the natural world surrounding them.

Perhaps no other country so embodies the word and concept of "eco-travel" as Costa Rica. The phenomenon of traveling to undeveloped places to do unconventional things seemed to enter our awareness at the exact same time in the late '80s that travel agents and ex-pats began raving about the raw beauty of "the Switzerland of Central America." On the narrow tropical isthmus of Costa Rica, eco-travel outfitters found the ideal mix of diverse ecosystems and sporty diversions, of Third World mystique and First World convenience.

Still, "eco-travel" is such a vague jellyfish of a word. Only in a place like Costa Rica does "eco-travel" gain context and sense. A place where 27 percent of the country's land is protected (the highest percentage of any nation on earth). A place where the wildlife of North and South America meet and mix. A place that occupies only .01 percent of our planet's landmass yet houses 5 percent of its diversity. When discussing travel to Costa Rica, you automatically precede words with "eco."

These days, the eco-travel opportunities seem limitless. In addition to simple walking, you can experience Costa Rica's biodiversity via horse, river raft, and sea kayak. Canopy tours are a local specialty: Participants secure themselves in

---

AT A GLANCE

TRIP LENGTH 8 days
PHYSICAL CHALLENGE 1 ② 3 4 5
MENTAL CHALLENGE 1 2 3 ④ 5
PRIME TIME December–April

PRICE RANGE (INDEPENDENT TRIP) $320
PRICE RANGE (OUTFITTED GROUP TRIP) $700
STAGING CITY San José, Costa Rica
HEADS UP Car break-ins are common, especially around San José

mountaineering harnesses, climb 90 feet up a hollow tree and onto a makeshift platform, and then glide, via a pulley and cable system, out over the teeming forest floor and onto the next platform. (FYI to my fellow Tarzan fans: Costa Rica really swings.)

Sample your eco options, then see Costa Rica by bike. When you pedal here, you move at a perfect pace. The deep, intricate landscape reveals itself layer by fascinating layer. You see buckets of flora, oodles of fauna. Mountain biking the outback convincingly proves that Costa Rica is the world's zoo.

Riders, like biologists, experience incredible diversity here. You can ride through a rain forest, knifing your shoulders through countless tendrils of lush greenery while howler monkeys make their loud, shrieking case that they are the most appropriately named species on Earth.

You can travel the remote southwest coast, riding from a vegetarian hippie enclave that teaches yoga on the sand, to beachfront pastures populated by floppy-eared-yet-somehow-dignified-looking Brahman cattle.

You can ride sidewalk-thin ribbons of asphalt deep into rural Costa Rica, from coffee plantations to pineapple groves. You can put away the map and just point your front wheel toward the smoke-belching pyramid of the Arenal Volcano—calling it a day at Tabacon Hot Springs, an oasis where steamy water gurgles into your pores while you marvel at plant leaves the size of pillowcases.

You can spin lazily into tunnels of green while sloths and toucans, wise in the minimal movement logic of the tropics, keep still and watch.

You can park your bike along a small, clear stream, than scamper—on all fours, up slippery rocks—to a hidden waterfall. The Feng Shui contentment engendered by this aesthetic waterfall will make you that much more entranced by the movements of the *lagartija Jesucristo*—the "Jesus Christ lizard," so called because it runs across water.

You can follow the Route of the Conquistadors: the path established by the Spaniards who caught a serious imperialist bug and explored Costa Rica in the 1560s. The route runs 285 miles and connects the Caribbean with the Pacific.

Unlike other Latin American countries explored by the 16th-century Spanish, Costa Rica was sparsely inhabited. It had always been a sort of no-man's-land between the Aztecs to the north and the Incas to the south. As such, Costa Rica's cultural history is relatively short. You'll find its soul not in its antiquities, but in its ecosystems.

Costa Rica is no longer a secret. International travelers penetrate deep into its wilds. But even in Costa Rica's high season, it's easy to escape your fellow tourists. Just throw a leg over a mountain bike, and disappear into the dense understory of the forest. Navigate the rugged roads that few first-world tourists can tolerate. Roll down the jungle's mystery trails, and just see what happens.

Opposite: When the cool, damp cloud forest loses its charms, drop down to warmer climes, where toucans (above) adorn the canopy. Overleaf: Crossing a suspension bridge along the Route of the Conquistadors, Central Costa Rica.

Chilly morning ride at 10,000 feet, highlands of central Costa Rica.

WHAT TO EXPECT

Costa Rica lies in the Central American tropics between Nicaragua and Panama. It operates on Central Standard Time. From North America, you can fly direct to Costa Rica from Houston or Miami (both flights take roughly three hours). Renting a car at the airport makes it easy to tote your bike all over the country and to travel spontaneously. Bike touring directly from the airport is another option, especially if you have lots of time. If you're planning on taking mass transit around Costa Rica (buses are cheap), you might not want to hassle with bringing a bike. Take cheer that most outfitters now rent bikes, and their fleets have improved significantly in the last few years: Brand-name bikes with front suspen-sions are no longer difficult to find. Most of the best rides are found in the Central Valley, not too far from San José. You can also find great rides a multi-hour car ride away, whether in the Arenal Volcano area or the Osa Peninsula in the far south-west. In general, the Pacific side is more moun-tainous and more preferable for mountain biking than is the Caribbean coast.

Costa Rica lacks an established mountain bike infrastructure. Unless you're riding only with an outfitter, bring your own tools, tubes, and parts. Recreation trails are few. Instead, you ride the dirt roads that connect small towns and trails that serve some kind of real-world purpose (that is, for game to hunt, for fruit pickers to reach their groves, and so on). If you want to ensure an entertaining, conscripted ride, hook up with an outfitter. If you enjoy exploring—and don't mind that dead-ends and wild-goose chases happen—set off on your own. (Don't worry: While theft is common in Costa Rica, violent crime is rare.) Costa Rica boasts an infinity of raw back roads, and independent travelers will never lack for new adventures.

The highlands of Costa Rica reach 11,000 feet, and the riding can be chilly at times. Mostly, however, you'll ride in warm, humid climes. Expect sweat and mud—and an attendant fear of touching your own used laundry. Most visitors hit Costa Rica during the dry season (mid-November to April), but many travelers prefer the rainy or "green" season, due to the verdant scenery and lower prices. The dry season all but guarantees sunny weather for biking, but the rainy season—especially October—isn't bad at all: The storms are usually short, and in the heat of the tropics, they're not unwelcome.

You can contact the Costa Rica Tourist Board at 800-343-6332 or www.tourismcostarica.com.

LODGING

Near Monteverde, stay in the affordable yet beautiful wooden *cabinas* of the Arco Iris Ecolodge (506-645-5067; email: arcoiris@racsa.co.cr) which offers breakfast and lively conversation in the five languages spoken by the propri-etor. On the Osa Peninsula, stay at La Llante Picante (see Outfitters and Bike Shops) or at the clean, inexpensive Oro Verde hotel (506-735-5241; email: oroverde@sol.racsa.co.cr).

THE RIDES

Muéco de Navarro is frequently called the best single ride in Costa Rica. The trailhead is in the town of Paraiso (about 30 miles southeast of San José) at Paraiso's "Guardia Rural" shed. A 20-mile mix of singletrack and dirt road, it begins with a scenic, rollicking downhill to the bottom of the Orosi River valley. From there, climb a series of different roads labeled Muéco de Navarro until cresting a hill at 3,280 feet. Then ride singletrack through coffee plantations and pine forests. For more information visit www.axioma.co.cr/mtb.

The Monteverde Cloud Forest Preserve located north of Puntarenas in the Tilaran Mountains (21 miles off the InterAmerican Highway), is one of the best known protected areas in the tropics. The Quakers of Alabama originally owned this 11,000 hectares of forest inhabited by 100 species of mammals, 400 species of birds, and 120 species of reptiles. One of the better trails runs through the Monteverde Preserve to the Childrens Rain Forest Preserve, covering 15 miles through dense primary rain forest.

THE SLOTH

Almost everyone who visits Costa Rica expects to see a sloth—two-toed or three-toed, it doesn't matter. Sloths can be difficult to spot, since they spend much of their time high in the trees. Also, their natural camouflage and lethargic behavior makes them resemble termite nests. But sloths do come to the ground on regular occasions. Indeed, sloths store up urine and feces for a week, descend to the ground, and dig a hole at the base of the tree with their stubby tails. They then defecate, urinate over the mess, and cover it all with leaves before reascending. Why they do this is unknown. One theory holds that they're fertilizing their favorite food trees.

to-bathtub-warm-ocean thing every bit as well as Hawaii. Enjoy beachside Manuel Antonio National Park via dolphin watching, deep-sea fishing, or nature hikes (506-777-1262; email: info@iguanatours.com). Then head to the convoluted green folds of mountains above town, and ride. Estrella Tour (see Outfitters) offers a number of guided rides in the area, including a 20-mile downhill that drops 4,500 vertical feet.

Riding the Route of the Conquistadors is a major accomplishment: It hosts a rigorous endurance race every October. Riders begin in the Pacific coast resort town of Puntarenas, navigate river canyons and high plateaus, crest at the 11,100-foot Volcan Irazu, then drop and undulate all the way to the Caribbean coast. Contact race organizer Roman Urbina 506-224-0163, fax: 506-224-9746; email:Roman@mountain bikecostarica.com.

Santa Rosa National Park, in the far northwest of Costa Rica, is exceptional in that it boasts dozens of miles worth of maintained trails. The dry tropical forest enclosed in the park's boundaries includes bats and tapirs, a pony-size mammal with a prehensile snout. Its beaches see the mass nestings of olive ridley turtles.

Turrialba riding includes some archeological sites as well as great sparkling pools begging you to jump in. Serendipity (see Outfitters) also runs guided tours from the San José airport to the beach.

OUTFITTERS AND BIKE SHOPS
Serendipity Adventures is based in the mtb-friendly town of Turrialba (about 45 miles east of San José).

Estrella Tour leads a full spectrum of rides near Quepos and Manuel Antonio, on the Pacific coast. Choose from a variety of beginner to expert-level rides, whether single- or multi-day. Highlights include explorations of indigenous settlements and hidden waterfalls.

Top: Transporting bikes along the 285-mile Route of the Conquistadors. Middle: Riding at 11,000 feet, rim of Irazu volcano. Bottom: Taking a break outside a store at a village in the northwest.

A good place to mix beach and biking is Manuel Antonio, a beautiful slice of tropics that does the jungly mountain-tumbling-down-

SERENDIPITY ADVENTURES

Serendipity de Costa Rica S.A.
Apdo. 76 CATIE
Turrialba, Costa Rica
800-635-2325
or
P.O. Box 2325
Ann Arbor, MI 48106
800-635-2325, 734-995-0111
www.serendipityadventures.com
$3,200 for 9 days

ESTRELLA TOUR

P.O. Box 305
Calle Central Quepos
Costa Rica
506-777-1286
Estrellatour@queposcostarica

RECOMMENDED READING

■ *FROMMER'S 2000: COSTA RICA* (1999.
$15.95. Macmillan.) A fine general guidebook.
■ *COSTA RICA'S NATIONAL PARKS AND
PRESERVES* (1999. $18.95. The Mountaineers.)
Offers detailed descriptions of natural areas.
■ *THE MOSQUITO COAST,* Paul Theroux (1996.
$13.95. Penguin USA.) A novel about an
American family that moves to the jungles of
Central America to start a new, purer life away
from "the oil companies, the car industry, big busi-
ness." They build a colony in a jungle outpost-in
Honduras, actually. But Theroux's description of
"cocoa-colored rivers" and "jungle plants crowding
against each other" fits Costa Rica perfectly. You'll
get a kick out of *The Mosquito Coast* if you've traveled at all in the tropics.

Bike transport Costa Rican style, aboard a banana boat.

Maui, Oahu, Molokai & Kauai

You knew about the frangipani-scented sea breezes and exotic birds flying over intricate lava formations. Now it's time to see the "kine" singletrack.

My friend Greg and I had just pedaled to a high point on Kauai's Powerline Trail. One look at the emerald vistas marching off to the horizon convinced us to declare a rest stop, to kick back with the fresh pineapple chunks we'd stored in Zip-Loc bags and just gaze at the flora of the "Garden Isle."

As the first dripping handfuls of pineapple oozed into our maws, a shaft of sunlight broke through the clouds about a mile away from us.

The first rays struck the edge of a natural amphitheater that framed a much taller triangular peak. As the clouds moved, sunshine washed slowly over the amphitheater. It lit up a staircase of smaller peaks in sequence—as an altar boy lights a row of candles—before finally revealing the glory of the master peak.

I was all but dumbfounded by the show, but Greg promptly broke the silence: "You know something? I bet if you fell off a cliff into the

Na Pali Coast State Park on Kauai's northwest coast is as close to ideal as many mountain bikers will ever come.

KAUAI

OAHU

PACIFIC

Honolulu

MOLOKAI

LANAI MAUI

▲ *Haleakala Volcano*

HAWAII

HAWAII

brush, it'd hurt, but it wouldn't kill you, you know?" Greg, a native of dry Southern California, was growing obsessed with Hawaii's almost comical overabundance of vegetation, especially on Kauai. "It'd be kind of cool, in fact, to just jump into it. You could wear a helmet and a ski suit to keep from getting scratched. Then just roll and roll down the mountainside and never get hurt!"

In Greg's defense, the greenery of Hawaii can be almost overwhelming. The Aloha State welcomes and seduces visitors with its frangipani-scented sea breezes and tropical warmth. Exotic birds fly over intricate lava formations. Sun-drenched wildflowers drink the spray of thundering waterfalls. An archipelago of swaying palms, white-capped surf, and long stretches of white sand, Hawaii tends to elicit starry-eyed "wows." Greg's use of a crazily violent metaphor to describe the lushness was actually quite original.

How on earth do you say anything new about Hawaii? What use of the word "paradise" hasn't been trotted out? What cheap temptation to call it "Fantasy Island" has been resisted? Mark Twain—who declared Hawaii to be "the loveliest fleet of islands that lies anchored in any ocean"—started the genre of Hawaii travel writing and Mark Twain should have retired it. The thousands of travel writers who have followed are only attempting a

double whammy of impossibility: conjuring utopia and topping Mark Twain.

Of course, Mark Twain never addressed the subject of mountain biking. Neither do many contemporary travel writers. Mountain biking sits low on Hawaii's sports totem pole. Surfing is the historical and spiritual big kahuna, and golf gets all the land and resources. The most attention biking gets is for the downhill volcano runs. Tour companies take visitors to the top of, say, Maui's 10,023-foot Haleakala Volcano, put them on 40-pound beach cruisers, instruct them never to get ahead of the slow-moving guides, and lead them cautiously downhill past diesel-spewing tour buses. It's a shame that this is considered great biking, because Hawaii's interior highlands beg for off-road riding.

Things are definitely improving. On Maui, superb, moist singletracks snake through lush forests on the flanks of volcanoes—and more trails keep getting built by Na Ala Hele, the state trail and access system. The lesser known island of Molokai now draws a constant stream of riders to Molokai Ranch, an mtb-oriented outfit spread over 54,000 tropical acres—a full third of the island. The Big Island of Hawaii features forest trails through timberlands and ferns, an intriguing

---

AT A GLANCE

TRIP LENGTH 7 days	PRICE RANGE (INDEPENDENT TRIP) $500
PHYSICAL CHALLENGE 1 2 ③ 4 5	PRICE RANGE (OUTFITTED GROUP TRIP) $1,000
MENTAL CHALLENGE 1 2 ③ 4 5	STAGING CITY Honolulu, Hawaii
PRIME TIME Anytime	HEADS UP Many routes veer into private land; ride with respect

mélange of green duff and black volcanic soil. Even Oahu, the site of Honolulu and Hawaii's thickest crowds, claims a large network of mtb-friendly singletrack.

The Hawaiian Islands represent the exposed peaks and submerged mountains of a great chain of extinct, dormant, or active volcanoes. Their eruptions have been, for the most part, as kind and gentle as Hawaii's beloved trade winds. Lava flows, not explosive cataclysm, have formed the topography. As a result, great rounded mountain masses characterize Hawaii, versus the steep cones of other volcanic areas. Mountain bike trails adhere well to the relaxed pitches.

America's 50th state is nothing like any of the other 49, and it also stands apart from other tropical mtb destinations. It combines island vibes with the First World's wherewithal to build trails just for fun. Unlike many tropical isles, Hawaii possesses big mountains (almost 14,000 feet) and lots of soft dirt (centuries and centuries of rain have leached the rocky bite out of the crust). Hawaii's unrivaled watersports have imbued it with a "see-no-limits" approach to outdoor sports that makes mountain bikers feel welcome. Its

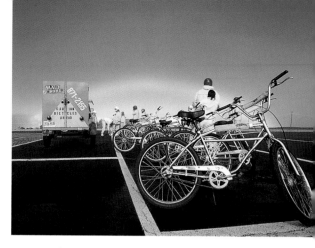

Preparing for the bicycle descent from Haleakala, at 10,023 feet, the largest dormant volcano in the world.

polyglot of cultures creates cuisine that makes mountain bikers feel contented and full.

Many of Hawaii's millions of tourists never travel much beyond the beach. They have no idea that inside the interior's deep emerald tangles reside the tropical fantasies that drew them to the South Pacific. With a mountain bike and a little sweat, you can experience Hawaii at its most raw—and do so alone.

Greg and I, for instance, were amply rewarded once we turned our back on Maui's

MAUI SUNBURN

If you somehow get a sunburn in Maui, Hawaiian mythology has an interesting explanation for it. Maui's giant dormant volcano, Haleakala, has long been a spiritual center for Hawaiian kahunas or priests. The summit is thought to be an energy vortex, a natural power point for magnetic and cosmic forces. Legend says that the goddess Hina was having problems drying her tapa cloth because the days were too short. Her son Maui, the prankish demigod after whom the island is named, decided to take matters into his own hands. One morn-

ing he went to the top of the mountain and waited for the sun. Maui braided a rope from his sister's pubic hair and as the sun came up over the mountain he lassoed the rays one by one and held on until the sun came to a halt. When the sun begged to be let go, Maui demanded that as a condition for its release it hereafter slow its path across the sky. The sun gave its promise, the days were lengthened, and the mountain became known as the House of the Sun.

Opposite: Sunrise on Haleakala ("House of the Sun"), Maui's giant volcano.

Mountain biker on the Munro Trail, Lanai.

coast and started pedaling into the rain forest. The path was so twisted that we could never see more than a hundred yards in front of us. The tree canopy darkened to a monochromatic hunter green. Mud coated our tires and painted Jackson Pollock tributes on our T-shirts.

Then, miles from our nearest fellow tourist, the rain forest opened up to reveal a roaring 50-foot waterfall. Clear, sparkling water fell musically into a supernaturally round pool. Cliffs carpeted with dripping ferns rose 300 feet above. We sat on a rock, dangling our feet in the water. Just as we finished our pineapple, the sun came out. I started to say something about paradise, then stopped in midsentence. The waterfall was saying the same thing, only louder, and I didn't want to interrupt.

WHAT TO EXPECT

Most visitors fly first to Honolulu (on the island of Oahu), then catch short flights from there to the other islands. Oahu, Maui, Molokai, the Big Island, and Kauai all boast excellent riding.

Mountain biking keeps growing in Hawaii, resulting in nicely developed trails, dependable service, and a good selection of rentals and accessories. The rides never get too crowded, yet they do bear substantial traffic. Erosion is a problem, especially when cyclists ride in the rain. Trail managers will definitely close eroded trails, so when it's wet, try to ride jeep roads instead of fragile singletracks.

Average temperatures differ very little from winter to summer. June through October is the hottest period, while rainfall is heaviest between December and March—neither extreme is worth worrying over. Hotel prices are lowest between April and mid-December.

The trade winds from the northeast sweep across the island for most of the year. They cause clouds to dump precipitation on windward sides, and keep lee sides relatively dry. The rain can be extremely heavy. Kauai's Powerline Trail, for instance, runs just a couple ridges over from the wettest place on earth—Kaawako Heiau, where 451 inches of rain fall every year. Prepare for mud: Bring dark socks, old jerseys, glasses that fully cover your eyes, and, most important, goop-specific tires.

The drier areas, on the other hand, contain sharp-edged lava rock and thorns. Be ready for flats: Bring a pump, extra tubes, and maybe even flat-fighters like Slime sealant. Trade winds keep mosquitos from becoming major pests, but it's still a good idea to rub some bug juice on uncovered limbs.

For general information, contact the Hawaii Tourism Authority (808-586-2550; www.hawaii. gov/tourism/). The state's trail gurus are at Na Ala Hele State Trails and Access Program (808-973-9782).

The northwest coast of Kauai is rife with rain forests, undulating terrain, and miles of doubletrack, singletrack, and dirt roads.

The Hawaii Bicycling League (808-735-5756 or email: mtnbike@aloha.net) also has information.

LODGING

Molokai Ranch (877-726-4656; www.molokairanch.com) houses guests in "tentalows": private tents perched on elevated platforms with queen beds and solar-heated showers.

Maui Kamaole (800-711-6284) offers affordable condos only minutes away from the Kamaole Beach Park. Amenities include air conditioning, color cable TV, VCR, telephone, washer and dryer, and fully equipped kitchen

Kokee State Park on Kauai (808-335-5871) contains a number of cabins on-site, enabling easy rides right from your door.

THE RIDES

MAUI

The Mamane and Waiakoa Loop trails in Maui's Kula Forest Preserve bring singletrack to the 7,000-foot-high flanks of Haleakala (literally "House of the Sun"), the largest dormant volcano in the world. The twisty trails get tight and technical in cedar forests, but the carpets of pine needles and smooth dirt invite jumping and other giddy behaviors.

OAHU

The Maunawili Trail is an all-singletrack out-and-back that's considered the most scenic ride on the island. While steep cliffs, waterfalls, and the blue Pacific beg for attention, keep your eye on the trail: This is a technical ride, loaded with

mandatory dismounts, water crossings, loose rocks, and sudden drop-offs. The trailhead is located at the first scenic lookout past the Pali tunnels on Hwy. 61.

KAUAI

Kokee State Park on Kauai is rife with rain forests and undulating terrain. And it's interlaced with singletrack, doubletrack, motorbike trails, and dirt roads-so many of them that it takes a few days to really ride it all.

OUTFITTERS AND BIKE SHOPS

Bike Hawaii offers daily bike adventures on Oahu, on both public and private lands. One of its tour guides is the author of two comprehensive trail books for the Hawaiian Islands.

Molokai Ranch offers all levels of rides on the island of Molokai. Less experienced riders can sample downhill rides, then catch a shuttle back. Advanced riders can do long loops connecting fragrant eucalyptus groves to the high cliffs overlooking Kalaupapa Peninsula. Or take a night tour with high-tech lights.

Island Biker is a full-service shop in the Maui town of Kihei; it's staffed with very enthusiastic, very knowledgeable mountain bikers. On Kauai, try Bicycle John.

BIKE HAWAII
P.O. Box 240170
Honolulu, HI 96824
877-MTB-RIDE
www.bikehawaii.com
$65 per day

MOLOKAI RANCH
P.O. Box 259
Maunaloa, HI 96770
877-726-4656
$75 per day
www.molokai-ranch.com

ISLAND BIKER
1279 S. Kihei
Kihei, HI 96753
808-875-7444

BICYCLE JOHN
3142 Kuhio Hwy.
Lihue, HI 96790
808-245-7579

RECOMMENDED READING

■ *MOUNTAIN BIKING THE HAWAIIAN ISLANDS,* John Alford (1995. $12.95. Ohana Publishing.) Written by a native rider, this is the best guidebook. It augments trail access information (for Hawaii, Maui, Molokai, Lanai, Oahu and Kauai) with photos and maps.

■ *HAWAII,* James Michener (1994. $7.00. Fawcett.) A historical novel charting the Islands' history from their volcanic origins to their emergence as a U.S. state.

Poli Poli Park, upcountry Maui, where the trails thread beneath the dense dark green canopy of rain forest.

Negril, Ocho Rios & the Blue Mountains

Unlike North America, riding here doesn't remove you from people; it enables you to meet them in strange places under sublime circumstances.

T here's a cow in the bougainvillea. Three pals and I bike right past it: a large, slow-witted domestic animal standing in the middle of a bush festooned with stunning purple-red blossoms. Have I been in Jamaica too long? Am I dreaming this? I look back. The cow returns my stare, its big blinking cow head framed by the bright flowers, looking for all the world like a label on some designer cheese. In America, the plants would have a gardener and the cow would have a pen. In Jamaica, there's a cow in the bougainvillea.

The dirt road takes us past pods of Jamaican boys playing in their yards. They recognize our tour guide, Rusty Jones, and urge him to catch some air on his bike. "Lift it! Lift it!" they shout with a lilt.

Continuing on, we engage a steep uphill. Brightly painted dwellings march up the slope toward a peak called Mount Airy. Through a pas-

Rusty's X-Cellent Adventures in Negril, the heart of mountain biking in Jamaica, offers beds, bikes, and more.

JAMACA

Montego Bay

Ocho Rios

Buff Bay

Negril

Blue Mountains

CARIBBEAN

Kingston

tel-pink house's window we can see a Jamaican mother sleeping, her baby curled in her arms. The next yard has a sign out front advertising tarot card readings. There are no people at the house, but a huge goat lounges on its steps.

We log a few miles under the hot sun before coming upon a woodsy copse. Leading into it is an unblemished red-dirt singletrack. We turn onto this soft carpet of chili powder, feeling exultant: Shade! Singletrack! Then we suddenly stop. A mango tree has peppered the ground with perfectly ripe juicy fruit. Barely pausing to rip the skin off, we devour mangoes until orange stains our cheeks and thick, ropy strings of fiber stick between our teeth.

The ride ends with a long haul back to Negril and the picturesque shacks peddling reggae tapes, jerk chicken, or Red Stripe beer. Near one of the shacks—I can't remember if it was the Love Zone, Culture Yard, Happy Bananas, or some other colorful name—a man points at our bodies, which by then are nothing more than smelly bags of sweat and heaving lungs, and laughs. "Rrrusstee!" he exclaims, the word rolling languorously off his tongue. "You steal the air from dere bellies!"

In North America, most mtb paths are playthings, existing in parks and recreation areas.

Trails generally bend away from humanity and its messy details.

In Jamaica, though, singletracks and doubletracks constitute tendrils of the region's nervous system, connecting a community's various functions and reflexes. It's dirt with a purpose, whether for cows to find greener pastures or sugarcane harvesters to commute to work. Riding here doesn't remove you from people; it enables you to meet them in strange places under sublime circumstances.

And the Jamaican people define "exotic." They came from Africa, but also England and Spain (which explains cities named Ocho Rios and Rio Grande). The children of whites and blacks are called "brownies." Bob Marley, son of a 50-year-old white military man and an 18-year-old black girl, was one. Brownies play at school with descendants of East Indians, Syrians, Chinese, French, and Portuguese Jews. Hence the national motto, "Out of Many, One People." Beneath the dreadlocks sit some unbelievable looking faces. I met one man who'd be a spitting image of the Sphinx if only his nose fell off.

All told, 2.5 million people inhabit the Connecticut-sized island. About half live in cities such as Kingston, Montego Bay, and Ocho Rios on the coast. The rural half occupy the mountains that

---

AT A GLANCE

TRIP LENGTH	6 days	PRICE RANGE (INDEPENDENT TRIP)	$400
PHYSICAL CHALLENGE	1 2 3 ④ 5	PRICE RANGE (OUTFITTED GROUP TRIP)	$1,000
MENTAL CHALLENGE	1 2 3 ④ 5	STAGING CITY	Kingston, Jamaica
PRIME TIME	December–April	HEADS UP	Kingston and Montego Bay contain many dangerous neighborhoods

Kingsley at Wesbes Bicycle Shop, Negril, Westmoreland, at the western end of Jamaica.

account for most of Jamaica's terrain. The highest range, situated on the eastern side, is the Blue Mountains, topped by 7,402-foot Blue Mountain Peak. Lesser mountains, with many transverse spurs, extend to the island's western edge.

The mountains—carpeted in thick vegetation and full of sharp limestone—are by no means as mtb-friendly as California's Sierra. Yet even in the jungle, trails do take hold. Cows, donkeys, goats, and, yes, slaves have stomped paths into the dirt for centuries. And most of the country's roads remain unpaved. On a mountain bike, you can penetrate Jamaica's undeveloped countryside and experience places inaccessible by any other mode of transportation. Mountain biking doesn't get the exposure that Jamaican pastimes such as beachgo-

ing and golf receive. But it should. If nothing else, a mountain bike makes for ideal transportation in the Caribbean—where the roads are rough and driving is a headache, but the scenery and weather are something close to divine.

Expect to see verdant trees covered with clusters of red poinciana and flaming jacaranda; to see the sun, like a burning ball of fire, disappear slowly below the western sky. Expect to hear birdsong: Jamaica contains 25 species and 21 subspecies that are found nowhere else on earth, and a total of 256 different birds. Expect to hear reggae. The sounds of Jamaica's best-known export issue from every nook. Houses with no doors, windows, or running water have blasters cranking. When out on a ride, you sometimes hear reggae booming through the woods in remote places where there's no habitation, much less electricity.

Reggae, of course, is one of Jamaica tourism's famed "three R's," along with rum and reefer. Another "R" that tourists don't always understand is Rastafari, an indigenous religion that emerged in Jamaica during the 1930s as a grassroots answer to social conditions and the irrelevance of white-oriented denominations. Rastafarianism —which teaches the redemption of blacks and their return to Africa, and advocates marijuana smoking as a sacrament for meditation—has been used as a cover by criminals, and as a publicity gimmick by pop musicians, but in its pristine form it is a valid faith that emphasizes the indwelling God Spirit in every person. Other

religions include Christianity, Judaism, Bahai, and Islam. It is said that there are more churches per square mile in Jamaica than anywhere in the world. The variety of houses of worship covers everything from centuries-old parish churches to the bamboo-and-zinc shacks of Revivalists.

This green mountainous island rising above the Caribbean has inspired reverence for its entire recorded history. When Christopher Columbus "discovered" Jamaica on his second voyage to the New World, he described it as "the fairest land mine eyes have ever seen." Ride a beachfront singletrack as waves thrum against the shore, and you'll know what he was talking about. Like many religions, though, Jamaican mtb worship requires some belief in things that aren't readily apparent.

The author puts Slime into his tubes at Rusty's. Thorns and coral rock cause flats.

ENGLISH vs. JAMAICAN

Jamaica calls English its official language and insists that motorists drive on the left. A recent survey revealed that almost 40 years after Jamaica officially became independent, 56 percent of its citizens still want to keep the British monarch as head of state. Still, this is the Caribbean, and some Eurocentric traditions seem much too formal and uptight. Handshakes, for instance. In lieu of them, Jamaicans tend to make a fist, lightly punch each other's knuckles, and say, "Respect." For newcomers, the process is longer: fist on top of fist, fist on bottom of fist, then the knuckle punch. According to a Negril local who called himself a witch doctor, the gesture means: "Glad

to meet, sad to depart, it hurts to hit, so do not fight."

Students of dialect maintain that the patois varies from parish to parish and even from yard to yard. Jamaica Talk is a synthesis of several influences: Old English and nautical terms such as "breadkind" and "catch to"; Spanish as in "shampata" from, *zapatos* (shoes); Irish dialect as in "nyampse" (a fool); African as in "duppy" (a ghost) or "nyam" (to eat), and American slang such as "cool" elaborated as "cool runnings" or "diss" as in disrespect. Rastafarian "I-dren" (brethren) have their own language and one word that you will hear frequently is "Irie" meaning good, happy, pleasant, or high.

Newcastle, in the Blue Mountains, where the clouds are constantly creating new shapes and shadows.

With only a couple of outfitters, few recreation trails, and a thorough lack of mtb guidebooks, mountain biking isn't simple here. Its appeal and rewards are much like the developing world itself: raw.

The joy of mountain biking this Third World island, I suppose, is made clear one day on a jaunt south of Negril. We're riding a singletrack that shadows an azure jag in the Caribbean called Homer's Cove. Because it's a beachfront on a well-touristed isle, we half expect to see a golf course. Instead, we encounter several cows. It's odd to be dodging pies as we pedal along the breathtaking shore, but we're happy with the arrangement. Cows, unlike golfers, are happy to share the fair soil of Jamaica.

WHAT TO EXPECT

Jamaica is the largest English-speaking island in the Caribbean: 600 miles south of Florida and less than two hours by plane from Miami. It is 146 miles long, between 22 to 55 miles wide, and has considerable variation in landscape from the coral sands and iron-laced cliffs of the shoreline, through coastal wetlands, plains, and highlands to the misty peaks of the Blue Mountains.

As with any Third World destination, self-reliance is rewarded. If you're bringing your bike, bring the tools to fix it, too. And don't forget spare tubes. Between copious thorns and coral rock, flats will happen. Hard-core Jamaican mountain bikers religiously put Slime or other flat-prevention additives into their tubes.

Trail riding usually involves technical challenges and some rock. Renting a bike from an outfitter makes a lot of sense. Plus, an outfitter has the local knowledge to negotiate private land and to find unmarked trails.

Jamaica has a maritime tropical climate.

The average daily temperature varies according to elevation from a high of 86°F at sea level to a low of 63°F in the mountains. The average annual rainfall ranges from 300 inches on the eastern slopes of the Blue Mountains to 230 inches in some parts of the south coast. Jamaica is rideable all year long. If you plan on spending time on the east coast or in the Blue Mountains, take account of the so-called rainy season, which extends from May to November with two peaks: May/June and October/November. Although this time of year is a little more humid than others, rain usually falls for short periods (normally in the late afternoon), and it's quite possible to enjoy sunshine for most of your visit. The peak tourist season runs from mid-December to mid-April, with Christmas and Easter the busiest weeks. The mountain bike trails, though, are never busy.

For general info, contact the Jamaica Tourist Board (800-233-4582; www.JamaicaTravel.com).

LODGING

Rusty's X-Cellent Adventures can house several guests in its octagonal tower on the outskirts of Negril. In addition to a complete bike shop, this architectural marvel has an open-air kitchen and dining room, breezy rooms with (discreet) outdoor showers, and a patio with four hammocks. (See Outfitters for info.)

Located directly on Negril's famous seven-mile beach are the Beach House Villas (800-NEGRIL-7; bhvillas@aol.com), offering fabulous views of the turquoise Caribbean. Compared to Negril's beachside luxury hotels, the prices are affordable.

THE RIDES

Expect a variety of textures—sandy backroad cruises, smooth descents down red-dirt avenues, wiggly navigations of crushed limestone powder, and ballsy thrashes down spiny coral-rock beds.

Catching air off a crashed plane's wing.

NEGRIL

Negril, home to Rusty's X-Cellent Adventures, is Jamaica's premier mountain biking region. Clinging to the waterfront, you can ride a singletrack on what was once a secret airstrip for drug smugglers; bonus points for catching air off a crashed plane's discarded wing. Or head up and inland to Jamaica's main plateau. There you'll find Rasta cowboys, riding horses as dreadlocks bounce against their shoulders, and swooping trails in lush valleys that could be in Montana were it not for the low-slung, huge-canopied shade trees called basidas.

OCHO RIOS

The Upton Trail starts from the perimeter road surrounding the Sandals golf course near Ocho Rios. Mixing root-filled gullies, paved roads, singletrack, and doubletrack, Upton is eight miles of fun, intermediate spinning. A highlight is the 200-year-old Spanish Bridge, which spans a scenic river and makes a nice rest stop. For more info, use the trail finder at www.mtbr.com.

In Jamaica singletrack is dirt with a purpose, whether for cows or bikers or sugarcane harvesters commuting to work.

The Dunn's River Falls ride, also near Ocho Rios, centers around falls that the early Spanish explorers somehow decided to climb. The ride climbs 1,500 feet above Ocho Rios to Murphy Hill. Then, looking down on the city and a gorgeous sea view, you descend through ferns to the spring feeding Dunn's River Falls. Drink up, then ride through woods while seeing how Ocho Rios got its name, "Eight Rivers." Follow at least one to the falls, and imagine climbing them in 16th-century gear.

The Rio Grande Valley, in the John Crow Mountains, is laced with paths. They parallel bubbling streams and bamboo forests, scale the sides of mountains, and meander through the fern-laden valley floor where one can find respite with a refreshing dip in a hidden waterfall or explore a tucked-away cave. But the trails are very challenging on bike; expect to do some walking and portaging.

BLUE MOUNTAINS

In the Blue Mountains, ride the road that goes up through Newcastle and down to Buff Bay. Beyond Hardware Gap and before you sweep down to Silver Hill is a beautiful, ever-changing

JAMAICA'S FAVORITE SWASHBUCKLER

Jamaica has always been swashbuckling. In the late 17th century, during English colonization, pirates ruled the Caribbean; one even rose high in Jamaica's early government. In the 1930s, swashbuckling actor Errol Flynn lived here. The fact that Ian Fleming wrote all his James Bond novels in the hills above Kingston seems fitting. *Dr. No*, set mostly in Jamaica, puts Bond against a backdrop of Cold War fears and Jamaica's surge toward independence.

As with most of Fleming's originals, the book of *Dr. No* is much darker than the film. Dispatched to the Caribbean to investigate another British agent's disappearance, Bond washes up on the island of Doctor No, a self-made genius with steel claws for hands, an army of thugs, and a clinical curiosity regarding the limits of human pain. Readers find gripping scenes throughout: Bond wrestles a squid, Bond lies still in bed while a poisonous centipede crawls all over his naked body. But just when James Bond comes close to earning our pity, he reunites with a babe named Honey Rider and frolics in the Jamaican surf.

vista over majestic hills—ever-changing because the clouds are constantly creating new shapes and shadows. Don't forget to stop and smell the fragrances of angels trumpets, eucalyptus, and wild ginger.

OUTFITTERS AND BIKE SHOPS

Rusty's X-Cellent Adventures, still the only pure mtb outfit in the nation, is a must-stop. Rusty Jones, an expat from Cleveland, has lived in Jamaica for more than 20 years. He started the Jamaican Mountain Bike Association, loans bikes to local teenagers, and knows every mtb route imaginable—from sugarcane fields to waterfall-blessed rivers, from emerald countryside to ancient caves. And his shop is equipped to handle high-tech bikes.

Safari Tours, in Ocho Rios, conducts bike tours of Dunn's River Falls, among other adventures.

RUSTY'S X-CELLENT ADVENTURES

Negril P.O. Box # 104
Westmoreland, Jamaica, West Indies
876-957-0155
www.webstudios.com/rusty
$500 for four days

SAFARI TOURS JAMAICA

Safari Tours, White River
P.O. Box 142, Ocho Rios
St. Ann, Jamaica, West Indies
876-795-0482
www.jamaica-irie.com/safari/
$55 per person per day

RECOMMENDED READING

■ *LONELY PLANET. JAMAICA* (2000. $17.95. Lonely Planet.) A fine general guidebook.
■ *DR. NO.* Ian Fleming (1958. $12.50. Macmillan.)

Top: The author slows down to the island's beat.
Above: Boston Beach, Port Antonio, on the east coast not far from the Blue Mountains.

Queensland

Like mountain bikers in general, Aussies encourage free exploration, approve of bruises, and smile at the concept of getting dirty.

When the overlords of mountain bike racing decided to hold the 1996 World Championships in Cairns, Australia, the decision seemed somehow appropriate. Sure, the pick went against the traditional grain: Most championships have been held near ski resorts, not the scuba diving paradise of the Great Barrier Reef. And never before had racers been required to journey to the Southern Hemisphere, to a place so maddeningly distant from the sport's American and European centers. But Cairns, located in the northeast of the state of Queensland, became one of the most popular and beloved World Championships in memory. Mountain biking—the outlaw cousin of road cycling, the scourge of well-to-do hikers and equestrians—was an ideal fit for a nation settled by convicts.

Foreign racers, many who brought to Australia *Mad Max*-fueled images of a dry, desolate

Kuranda train station, just outside Cairns and close to Queensland's Cedar Park Rain Forest.

Cape York Peninsula

SOUTH PACIFIC

Great Barrier Reef

Cairns

Great Dividing Range

QUEENSLAND

Brisbane

wasteland, were stunned by Queensland's natural beauty. Above the aquamarine waters pulsing around the reef, they discovered mountains and rain forests laced with singletracks. The more they rode, the more the racers fawned over Cairns, the anti-ski area. The World Championships venue boasted the long, serpentine trails of past venues, but none of the scenery-marring chairlifts and gravel snowcat roads. Once the racers departed the start area, they were in the woods—where oddly plumed birds screeched, Australia's world-record earthworms (six feet long) turned the soil, and the scissoring of eucalyptus leaves sounded hauntingly like the hiss of the local taipan (a deadly snake). Cairns gave the championships a raw, primal feel that hearkened back to mountain biking's earthy beginnings.

As much as any Australian state, Queensland encourages offroad pedaling. Not only does it offer outrageously beautiful landscapes, but it also lays claim to the island continent's most hospitable weather. Roughly bisected by the Tropic of Capricorn, Queensland ranges from tropical (hot and humid) and subtropical (warm and somewhat humid) in the north to temperate (moderate in temperature and humidity) in the south. Queensland's year-round warm and sunny climate has earned it the nickname "The Sunshine State," although it also receives adequate rainfall: 90 percent of Queensland gets at least eight inches of rain per year. As a result, Queensland has the largest livable area of any Australian state.

What's more, Queensland is riddled with parks and preserves. Its tip, the cone-shaped Cape York Peninsula, alone has nine national parks with areas greater than 2,470 acres. Along with rain forest, vegetation zones include tropical grasslands, heathlands, 4,000-foot mountains, dry outback, and mangroves. The forests along the coast have been designated a World Heritage site.

Little wonder, then, that Queensland also hosted the 1997 Eco-Challenge, the notorious multisport endurance race. The mountain bike segments highlighted Queensland's stunning diversity: The adventure jocks pedaled out of the hilly outback around Kirrama and toward the rolling farmland meadows of the Atherton

Overleaf: Sunrise over Dunk Island, Great Barrier Reef.

AT A GLANCE

TRIP LENGTH 9 days

PHYSICAL CHALLENGE 1 2 ③ 4 5

MENTAL CHALLENGE 1 2 ③ 4 5

PRIME TIME March–November

PRICE RANGE (INDEPENDENT TRIP) $450

PRICE RANGE (OUTFITTED GROUP TRIP) $600–$1,000

STAGING CITY Brisbane, Australia

HEADS UP The outback, where women still face discrimination and hitchhikers sometimes disappear

Tablelands. In between stood the rain forest, where numerous river crossings and mud bogs humbled riders—with wide-planked wooden bridges grabbing tires and hurling pilots from the saddle. They rode beneath otherworldly vegetation such as the wait-a-while, nature's answer to barbed wire, which dangles in long vines from the canopy of trees. It can cause severe lacerations and will easily pull riders from their bikes if it catches in their clothing. Or how about the Tar Tree and the Stinging Tree? The sap from the Tar Tree blisters skin on contact and can blind you if rubbed into your eyes. The Stinging Tree, if brushed against, injects tiny hollow filaments that allow air to reach nerve endings, causing excruciating pain for up to two weeks after exposure. While there is no way to remove the stingers, people have been known to burn off the affected area of skin using kerosene or hydrochloric acid.

Chances are, you'll easily avoid such nasty plants. We mention them here because they add to Australia's bizzare, almost absurd, lore. This is a country, after all, that combines British affectations with Mongolia's open spaces. Australia claims ranches the size of Belgium, and a school district the size of France. There's the unique settlement history, because leading social reformers in 1780s England assumed that the best way to eliminate crime was to remove criminals from society—even if it meant sending them to a distant island on the other side of the equator.

And no country on earth owns such an odd collection of wildlife. About 70 percent of Australia's birds, 88 percent of its reptiles, and 94 percent of its frogs exist nowhere else on the planet. Queensland riders may catch a glimpse of the elusive cassowary. If you do, you should keep your distance—these large flightless birds have been known to disembowel a man with one kick from their strong legs. Certainly you'll see Australia's famous marsupials. The 50 species of kangaroo are led by the large red or gray kangaroo, which may stand as high as 7 feet and can leap up to 30 feet. The wallaby, bandicoot, wombat, phalanger, and koala look as foreign as they sound. They're outweirded only by the primitive, egg-laying mammals known as monotremes. One of them, the platypus, a zoological curiosity, is an aquatic, furred mammal with a bill like that of a duck and with poisonous spurs. Australia has two species of crocodile, the smaller of which is found in inland fresh waters. The giant, fierce saurian crocodile of the northern coastal swamps and estuaries attains lengths of 20 feet. About 100 species of venomous snakes are found in Australia. The nation's waters contain some 70 species of shark, including great whites, and the Queensland lungfish, which is sometimes called a living fossil, for it breathes with a single lung instead of gills.

Of course, Queensland's hosting of the Eco-Challenge and the mountain bike World Championships was hugely overshadowed by the 2000 Olympics in Sydney. Many Aussies don't even remember the Cairns event or the praise it won. And who can blame them, really? Mountain biking occupies only a tiny part of the nation's sporting interest, and it may never attain the adoration and mainstream popularity of rugby,

Queensland hosted the 1996 World Championships (opposite) and the 1997 Eco-Challenge (above).

cricket, tennis, surfing, or swimming. Still, offroad riding is respected and well received in Australia simply because it is a sport played outside. Australia, see, has been called a nation of hedonists. Aussies certainly take every advantage of their temperate climate to spend as much time as possible outdoors. Barbecues are the preferred mode of eating—so much so that roadside rest areas offer coin-operated gas grills.

Get out there on a bike. See Queensland's weird wonders by day. Or saddle up as the final rays of sunlight penetrate the jacaranda foliage heavy with lavender flowers, and the first fruit bats arrive to feast on ripe mangoes: Night riding has become increasingly popular here, for Queensland shares the dependable weather of such U.S. night-riding hotbeds as California and Florida. Our sport will soon flourish here. Aussies who take a long enough recess from golf and water sports to try riding discover that mountain biking perfectly suits the national culture. Both sports allow free exploration, approve of bumps and bruises, and smile at the concept of getting dirty.

THE ABORIGINES

Before the British started sending their convicts to Australia, Queensland was home to 30 percent of all Australian Aborigines. Clashes between settlers and Aborigines became common and violent. At least 20,000 Aborigines died in the fighting, compared with 1,000 Europeans. European diseases also took a toll on the Aborigines. Thankfully, the settlers couldn't kill Aboriginal culture.

The oldest music in Australia is the music of the Australian Aborigines. In Aboriginal societies, music plays a central role in both social and sacred life. During social gatherings called corroborees, singing and dancing provide the major form of entertainment.

In sacred ceremonies, songs serve as the vital link to the realm of Aboriginal spirits called Dreamtime. The Aborigines believe that, long ago, the Dreamtime spirits sang songs that created all living things on earth. Today, these songs are sung in sacred ceremonies to ensure the survival and propagation of all plant and animal life. Sure, it's a hard concept to swallow—this singing of all matter into existence. But even the most traditional, least imaginative Westerner can appreciate the Aborigines' reverence for dreams. Anyone who travels across the world to pursue mountain bike fantasies should understand the meaning of the old Aborigine saying: "He who loses his dreaming is lost."

WHAT TO EXPECT

The Great Dividing Range, a sprawling system of mountain ranges running the length of the state from north to south, separates Queensland into four regions: the eastern plains, islands, and reefs of the coast; the eastern highlands; the western plains; and the northwestern uplands. The eastern coast is notable for its fine beaches and excellent farm land. Its most extraordinary feature is the coral reef chain of the Great Barrier Reef, which extends about 1,200 miles from north to south.

You might want to bring your own bike, especially if you're a gearhead. Aussie shops and outfitters offer quality rentals, but many are a few years old: Instead of today's 24- and 27-speed models, you'll see many 21-speeds. Bike touring is generally safe along the coast; in the outback, you could be figuratively crushed by the great distances and even literally crushed by the giant "road trains"—gargantuan trucks towing three tractor trailers. If you want to ride a lot of Queensland singletrack in a relatively short time, a road trip is preferable to bike touring.

Most of the best rides take place near the coast. You'll see mountain bikers about, and the shops you'll visit will be able to handle most any problem. But don't expect a Moab-like profusion of bike shops. Be as prepared as you can be, especially for mechanical problems, because you may not see a host of good samaritans in the depths of the rain forest.

As for weather, Queensland is hospitable almost all year, though temperatures can climb into the 90s during Australia's December–February "summer." Finally, realize that Australia is a heavily wired country, and is perhaps best researched via the Internet.

For general info on the Land Down Under, call Australia Tourism's U.S. number (800-369-6863) or the Queensland Government Travel Centre in Brisbane (07-221-6111).

There's far more to Australia than sheep, but grazing flocks are—for foreigners, at least—a national symbol.

LODGING

Near the center of Cairns proper is the moderately priced Flying Horseshoe Motel (61-070-513-022).

To stay close to Queensland's rain forest, journey just outside Cairns to Kuranda. There you'll find the Cedar Park Rainforest Resort (61-070-937-077), which is so secluded that ambient noise means the gurgling of the Clohesy River, wind in the trees, or the screech of sulfur-crested cockatoo.

In Brisbane, the Tower Mill Motor Inn (61-07-832-1421) is an affordable place with nice views from the balconies off its rooms.

Near Cairns, Queensland. Mtb suits the national culture: free exploration plus bumps, bruises, and dirt.

Youth hostels present another option. Despite the name, they welcome travelers of any age, so long as you don't mind sharing kitchen facilities and dormitory-type rooms. For a list of Queensland hostels, call 61-07-236-1680.

THE RIDES

The World Championship Downhill Course in Cairns is a kick. It pogos over technical wooden berms, rattles down a rocky singletrack, blasts a high-speed section down an old logging road (on which racer Toby Henderson reached 47 mph), rips across the forest floor, and hits a "phat" jump. Extreme sports icon Sean Palmer called it the world's best downhill. The Worlds cross-country track is great, too.

Toohey Forest, near Brisbane, is laced with dozens of fine paths. Expect a color contrast between green gum trees and red dirt. A signature technical trail leads from a rocky outcrop toward a cemetery: It's called The Death Stare.

Gap Creek Reserve, also located near Brisbane, blends intermediate-level doubletrack with narrow ribbons of challenging singletrack. Look for the Lantana Downs trail in particular, a twisty test piece boasting several drops off rocky ledges.

OUTFITTERS AND BIKE SHOPS

Dan's Mountain Biking has all the right credentials: Dan was the mountain bike course designer and leg coordinator for the 1997 Eco-Challenge Race. It leads trips for lower intermediates as well as experts, and takes riders to both the World Championship courses and secluded watering holes.

Bike 'n' Hike Mountain Bike Tours operates farther north, in the tropical rain forest around Port Douglas and Mowbray Valley (home to spectacular Mowbray Falls). Choose from a variety of trip difficulties and lengths.

Pro-Am Cyclery located in the Albany Creek region of Brisbane, is a premier shop: It sells the very best gear, services anything wheeled, and reminds patrons that "cycling is not just a sport or recreation, it's a lifestyle!" In Cairns, try Trinity Cycle Works.

DAN'S MOUNTAIN BIKING TOURS

20 Shannon Drive
Cairns 4870, Australia
61-07-40330128
www.cairns.aust.com/mtb/
$70 per person per day

BIKE 'N' HIKE MOUNTAIN BIKE TOURS

Mowbray Valley
North Queensland, 4871
61-7-3876-4644
www.greatbarrierreef.aus.net/bikenhike/
$70 per person per day

PRO-AM CYCLERY

720 Albany Creek Road
Albany Creek, Brisbane, Australia
61-7-3264-4593
www.Pro-Am.com.au

TRINITY CYCLE WORKS

40 Aplin Street
Cairns, Australia
61-07-40515380
Oliver@trinitycycles.com.au

RECOMMENDED READING

■ *CYCLING THE BUSH—THE BEST RIDES IN AUSTRALIA,* Sven Klinge (1996. $18.95. Hill of Content Publishing Co. www.jub.com.au/books/productlist/productlist.html) A comprehensive guide to off-road cycling Down Under, ranging from short one-day trips to extended overnight expeditions in remote and rugged wilderness areas.

■ *GREATER BRISBANE'S BEST BIKE RIDES,* a booklet at the tourism office, describes 29 rides for both road and mountain bikes in and around Brisbane. Contact: 61-7-3844-1144; benbiq@ozemail.co. You can also find a variety of Australia trail descriptions at www.mtbr.com.

Australia's gray kangaroo stands as high as seven feet and can leap up to 30 feet.

■ *THE SONGLINES,* Bruce Chatwin (1988. $13.95. Penguin USA.) A story of ideas in which two companions, traveling and talking together, explore the hopes and dreams that animate them and the people they encounter. The book asks and tries to answer these questions: Why do wandering people conceive the world as perfect, whereas the sedentary always try to change it? Why have the great teachers—Christ or the Buddha—recommended the Road as the way to salvation? Why is man the most restless, dissatisfied of animals? Mountain bikers, who may know a thing or two about these mysteries, will enjoy Chatwin's take.

■ *LONELY PLANET AUSTRALIA* (2000. $24.95. Lonely Planet.)

The Redwood Belt

These verdant, moss-weeping, evergreen-needle-carpeted wonderlands inspired the sport of mountain biking. And the cradle still rocks.

Two mtb friends—let's call them the Hippie and the Dog, and I were pumped to point our car north on U.S. Hwy. 101. In or on the car were CDs we all enjoyed, chocolate-covered espresso beans, a complete selection of tools and clothes, mountain bikes in good working order, and a fair amount of eager anticipation. For one, we were taking our first mtb road trip together—a hedonistic blend of travel and riding that would cement our friend-

ship in ways that we couldn't quite articulate (and being insensitive adult males, would never bother to). For two, we were departing Southern California for Northern California. That was our grail: to journey from our hardscrabble, sunbaked, cacti-strewn trails to the verdant, moss-weeping, evergreen-needle-carpeted wonderlands of the Redwood Belt. To ride trails that inspired the very sport of mountain biking, gave rise to its boom, and still tickled many of its best

Redwood National Park, near Prairie Creek State Park at the north end of the 200-mile-long Redwood Belt.

brains. To experience the once and forever spiritual nexus.

Our first stop was Prairie Creek State Park, located between Arcata and the Oregon state line. A storm had polished the skies the day before, and bright sunshine bathed the trailhead. Mounting up, we rode into a birch forest where light floated in on dreamy, gauzy strips. Although we hadn't come for trees as puny as birch, we stopped and shot lots of photographs. Then we rattled down to a huge open expanse of beach and seagrass—a famous feeding ground for Roosevelt elk. We snapped more pictures there. Then we encountered shimmering creek crossings; creeks being rare in Southern California, we burned still more film.

After quite a bit of uphill slogging, we reached the ride's highlight: a huge redwood grove lined with a glorious, five-mile, downhill singletrack. Once there, we promptly dismounted and began walking our bikes—it was simply too dark to ride. We'd spent so much time shooting photos that the afternoon had evaporated on us, as afternoons will do in these parts. Stumbling down the perfect cycling trail in the gloom, we realized (with a pain that still lingers five years later) that few places on earth are darker than a redwood forest after 6 P.M. in November.

And few places on earth are better to ride during daylight hours. Perhaps no species loves the mulchy redwood ecosystem as much as the local banana slugs do, but mountain bikers are right up there. The smells are delicious. The scents of bay leaves, redwood bark, and assorted decomposing things mix together to evoke the sweet, spicy fragrance of astringent. It's quiet, too, interrupted only by birdsong and breezes. If you try, you can almost hear the leaves mold and the whisper of the earth as it spins on its axis. Best of all is the dirt. Tacky, soft, and largely free of rocks and roots, it lays gently on winding, rolling trails. Mtb tires match it molecule for molecule, providing predictable steering and superb traction. When you ride redwood glades, you hug the dirt like a banana slug hugs dirt.

To a redwood, you're little more significant than a slug. *Sequoia sempervirens* can live to be 2,000 years old. Found only in Oregon and California, redwoods are the tallest living things on earth. They stand more than 300 feet above the forest floor and occupy roughly the same surface area as a starter home. In Humboldt Redwoods

Prairie Creek State Park

• **Arcata**
Humboldt National Redwood Forest

CALIFORNIA

• **Mendocino**

Marin County

PACIFIC

• **San Francisco**

• **Santa Cruz**

AT A GLANCE

TRIP LENGTH 8 days	PRICE RANGE (INDEPENDENT TRIP) $350
PHYSICAL CHALLENGE 1 2 ③ 4 5	PRICE RANGE (OUTFITTED GROUP TRIP) $1,200
MENTAL CHALLENGE 1 ② 3 4 5	STAGING CITY San Francisco, California
PRIME TIME April–October	HEADS UP Hikers and equestrians are often hostile to mountain bikers

Among the redwoods the smells are delicious, it's quiet and best of all, the dirt is tacky, soft, and free of rocks and roots.

State Park, we (the Hippie, the Dog, and I) actually rode up to the biggest tree in the world, officially named the Giant Tree. It measures 363 feet high and lists a circumference of 53 feet, 2 inches. In other words, riding your mountain bike around the bark of this one single tree would require your 26-inch tire to make 24 full revolutions.

Humongous redwoods supplied much of the lumber that built San Francisco following the Gold Rush. When naturalist John Muir explored Northern California in the late 19th century, redwoods gave him such a profound sense of shelter that he traveled with only a bedroll and a sack of

bread crumbs. The majesty of the redwoods helped convince Muir to found the Sierra Club, which in turn would protect the trees that had protected him. Tantalizing redwood forests loomed outside the windows of Mount Tamalpais High School, the Marin County institution attended by several of the iconoclasts credited with creating the sport of mountain biking. Redwoods withheld laughter in the early 1970s as rabble-rousers riding clunkers with balloon tires amassed scar tissue in an ongoing quest to develop nimble, lightweight bikes that could withstand the rigors of forested terrain.

Obviously, the quest succeeded. Mountain bikes now trundle across every corner of the globe. Yet their birthplace has never quite been topped as a place to ride. The snaking, soft dirt trails still respond better to skilled bike handling than to violent manipulations of suspension systems. The redwoods' old-growth spacing keeps trails tidy and protects them from the marauding vegetation that would swallow them. The coastal fogs that have nurtured redwood groves for centuries, plus temperatures hovering between 40 and 80°F, make for invigorating spinning conditions. Even in the hilly or dry spots where redwoods don't grow, the Northern California coast offers compelling scenery and topography. In

Opposite: To a redwood, which can live to be 2,000 years old, you're little more significant than a banana slug.

BURLY DROPPINGS

Many old-growth redwood groves have been spared thanks to spotted owl migrations and environmental activists' decisions to chain themselves to and/or live in the branches of the trees. Still, redwood lumber finds its way to Northern California gift shops. The explanation has to do with "burls," wartlike growths that spring up on redwoods' trunks. When these two-foot-long blemishes are cut or fall off, artisans carve them into every touristy knick-knack imaginable. There are burl clocks, burl end tables, and, especially, burl sculptures of Bigfoot.

short, you can do no bigger favor to your mountain biking self than to road trip the Redwood Belt, moving leisurely from one cathedral-like trail to the next.

Start the journey in Santa Cruz, near the redwoods' southern terminus. A surf mecca and college town, Santa Cruz wears its bohemian heritage proudly. While the Bay Area becomes overwhelmed with dot.com money and mores, Santa Cruz cleaves to older California virtues such as environmentalism and recreation. Everyone rides bikes, all the time. The town's vibrant velo culture embraces single speeds, cruisers, cyclo-cross, and tandems. The streets are full of them. Normal mountain bikes, meanwhile, escort their owners directly from art galleries, coffee emporiums, and head shops to redwood sanctuaries both tidy (the lovely Nisene Marks State Park) and ragged (the unmarked maze of looping singletracks abutting the University of California-Santa Cruz campus).

Continue north toward the Bay Area, stopping for at least a day at El Corte de Madera Creek Open Space Preserve (see The Rides). Leave your heart in San Francisco—your lungs, too—with urban assaults on the trails of Golden Gate Park and the Presidio. Cross the Golden Gate bridge to Marin County, where wealthy, influential hikers have managed to bar mountain bikers from many singletracks. Prepare to dislike Marin, only to find that the fireroad ascents up

Mount Tamalpais challenge you with dramatic pitches and entertain you with moody forests and, at the summit, outrageous views of the Pacific Ocean and San Francisco Bay.

Keeping the saltwater close by and on your left, head toward Mendocino and a cluster of state parks (highlighted by mtb-friendly Skyline Park). As the SUVs give way to logging trucks, look for evidence of Bigfoot. Around the flannel-shirted environs of Garberville, look for evidence that you haven't time-traveled back to the 1980s.

Reacquaint yourself with microbrews and the Internet in Arcata, a hemp-flavored college town, its shores pounded by gargantuan waves that apparently began growing right after leaving Japan. Continue from there to the trip's northern terminus at Prairie Creek State Park, where—again—it pays to start riding before the sun gets horizontal.

Whether you hit it rolling north or south, it's absolutely essential to visit Humboldt Redwoods State Park. The Giant Tree, the largest redwood on earth, is only a small part of the park's lure. A bigger enticement is the ride up Grasshopper Peak, which tilts abruptly out of the forest duff. It's a steep grind, and it lasts a while: The elevation change (from 300 to 3,379 feet) is as large as any you're likely to pedal in the redwoods.

But after an initial bout of small-ring mash-

FLOTSAM AND JETSAM

Majestic groves of redwoods lend dignity and grace to California's coast—which apparently needs all the dignity and grace it can get. According to the *Contra Costa Times*, the relatively clean-seeming California coast acts as a magnet to heinous amounts of garbage. Indeed, a recent cleanup netted 251 tons of trash and nearly 21 tons of recyclables. While cleaning the beaches of dis-

carded flotsam and jetsam, volunteers vie to find the weirdest objects, with the winner taking home a $500 prize. They've found bottled love letters, a carved pumpkin full of eggs, false teeth, and more. One volunteer won the $500 prize for finding a gravestone— from San Antonio, Texas. It makes you wonder if the tallest trees on earth constitute a big enough fence.

Pacific Ocean from High Bluff Coastal Drive, Redwood National Park, northern California.

ing, you come to a junction with Johnson Trail Camp singletrack. If you're like the Hippie, the Dog, and me, you rest on a downed redwood whose size and violent crash evoke a train wreck. You take stock of your Redwood Belt surroundings. The ferns and mosses slithering across valley floors and up canyon walls. The moist and molding forest floor. The damp air. The dim light, for the sun is but a distant, harmless thing.

Searching for metaphor, you proclaim that a redwood forest is nature's crawl space. Sure, you should describe the redwoods with words

more honorable than "crawl space." But there isn't time. The Hippie and the Dog are already plunging down the velvety ribbon of Johnson Trail Camp, and you promptly follow—enjoying a downhill so aesthetically perfect it almost excuses the tragic bungling of Prairie Creek's redwood-lined descent.

Almost.

WHAT TO EXPECT

As far as mountain bikers are concerned, Northern California's Redwood Belt stretches

Top: Foxglove (Digitalis), Redwood Creek watershed, northern California coast. Above: Marin County, miles of singletrack connecting stands of redwood and Douglas fir to sweeping sunlit meadows.

In the southern part of the Redwood Belt, long, hot summers can produce hard, scrabbly surface conditions and hamper traction. Further north, summer temperatures range between 40 and 75°F. Mosquitoes loiter in the wetter areas. Winter is wet throughout the Redwood Belt, with some portions getting 50 inches of rain or more (snow is rare at the redwoods' gentle altitudes). Midwinter rains generate deep mud and rushing streams that create new and interesting challenges and hazards. Trails may become impassable due to landslides, fallen trees, or flooding.

Because the redwoods do such an effective job of screening out sun, bring eyewear with light-colored lenses. Seriously, the sun doesn't make much of an impact unless it's directly overhead. Twilight barely happens, so bring lights if riding late in the day. Finally, keep in mind that poison oak flourishes in the shadow of the redwoods. Be careful going to the bathroom or doing anything else off trail.

For general information, contact California's tourism board (www.gocalif.ca.gov). To find information about camping and cycling in the parks, visit the Redwood National and State Parks Electronic Visitor Center (www.nps.gov/redw) www.nps.gov/redw).

LODGING

Big Basin Redwoods State Park (408-338-8860 or 800-874-TENT), a fine place to ride coastal redwoods not far from Santa Cruz, offers a couple of overnight options: standard campground facilities or space in a tentlike cabin.

For an actual roof near Santa Cruz's trails, go to Point Montara Lighthouse Hostel (415-728-7177), an older but charming building that caters to adventure travelers. Ask for the Watch room.

Located in Garberville near the Avenue of the Giants section of Redwoods National Park, the Benbow Inn (800-355-3301; 707-923-2124) is a venerable (built in 1926) and upscale way to

north from Santa Cruz through the Bay Area and up to Prairie Creek State Park. It's a 200-mile-long corridor that pushes as much as 50 miles inland but mostly shadows the Pacific coast.

Close to San Francisco, ride safely and carefully—not just to protect yourself, but to protect your sport's reputation. One dumb yahoo careening down the trail and scaring hikers and equestrians can do untold damage. Many singletracks are already feeling usage pressures: If the rangers who govern them are compelled to agree with persnickety hikers that mountain biking is dangerous, we could lose fine trails.

enjoy California's so-called "Lost Coast." Amenities include a library of over 250 films and wood-burning fireplaces.

THE RIDES

El Corte de Madera Creek Open Space Preserve contains 36 miles of multi-use trails a few dozen miles south of San Francisco. Its upper ridges provide views of the Pacific, but its heart is its deep basin: the lower you go, the more redwoods will squeeze out evergreens. To maximize singletrack, ride Manzanita to Timberview to Giant Salamander to Methuselah to South Leaf to Virginia Mill before returning on Fir.

Bolinas Ridge is one of the few Marin County classics available to law-abiding riders. It mixes towering redwoods, manzanita-covered ridges, twisty paths, sweeping descents, and land's-end views of Tomales Bay.

Annadel State Park, near Santa Rosa, is what Marin County should be: miles of crisscrossing singletrack connecting thick stands of redwood, bay, and Douglas fir to sweeping meadows. Annadel's comparative rockiness is more than compensated by scenic marshes and twisty trails—the best of which are South Burma, North Burma, Channel, and Spring Creek.

OUTFITTERS AND BIKE SHOPS

Marin Off-Road Mountain Bike Tours offers a number of supported tours in the Marin County area, including one called Four Climbs Happiness, which gains more than 5,300 feet of ascent—plus subsequent gobs of descent.

The Bike Trip in downtown Santa Cruz not only excels at servicing bikes; it also serves as the alma mater of a renowned mountain bike writer: Mike Ferrentino, whose curmudgeonly magazine columns on bike shop life ("Mr. Surly Wrench" and "The Grimy Handshake") gave mechanics a voice in the mainstream.

Mount Tam Cyclery performs shop duties in the Marin County town of San Anselmo.

MARIN OFF-ROAD MOUNTAIN BIKE TOURS
P.O. Box 622
Sausalito, CA 94966-0622
415-332-3262
$80 per day

THE BICYCLE TRIP
1127 Soquel Ave.
Santa Cruz, CA 95060
831-427-2580

MOUNT TAM CYCLERY
29 San Anselmo Ave.
San Anselmo, CA
415-258-9920

RECOMMENDED READING

■ *MOUNTAIN BIKING NORTHERN CALIFORNIA'S BEST 100 TRAILS,* Fragnoli and Stuart (2000. $18.95. Fine Edge.) As comprehensive a guidebook as its title suggests; its Redwood Belt coverage is slightly weighted toward Santa Cruz and the Bay Area.

■ *THE WILDERNESS WORLD OF JOHN MUIR,* edited by Edwin Teale (1954. $11.95. Houghton Mifflin.) Recounts Muir's Northern California adventures in his own words.

North & South Islands

*Few countries can match the geographical diversity here,
where subtropical rain forests sprout less than
a hundred miles from glaciers.*

New Zealand's most famous fruit, the kiwi, is not endemic to the nation's two remote islands in the Southern Hemisphere. Also known as the Chinese gooseberry, the kiwi was imported from, yes, China. Yet ever since they dreamed up the new name in the 1950s, New Zealanders have held the fruit dear—never mind if its startling green tangy flesh is encased in an unappetizing fuzzy, brown, suede-like skin. These days New Zealand produces about two-thirds of the world's kiwifruit. Natives collect the discarded skins and sew them into pillowcases. More interestingly, cunning mountain bikers use kiwi skins to patch the holes in their tire punctures.

Is this ingenious synergy of local resource and sport reason enough to visit New Zealand? No, not even remotely. But it does speak to New Zealand's appealing outdoorsiness. Here—in one of earth's cleanest, greenest triumphs of geo-

Near Wanaka, Otago Province, South Island, just east of the Southern Alps.

graphical diversity—the land always seems to provide.

When stating the size of New Zealand (103,736 square miles), geographers invariably compare it to either the United Kingdom or Colorado. Oddly, it's like a combination of both—an island nation with breathtaking peaks, clear air, multitudinous sheep, and good beer (no, that doesn't mean Coors). New Zealand is actually two islands—the aptly named North Island and South Island. Its 3.6 million people are somewhat clustered: three quarters of them live on North Island, a majority near Auckland; South Island is largely rural.

Mountains occupy 70 percent of the landmass. The most famous range, the Southern Alps, has a derivative-sounding name, but these glaciated, 11,000-plus-foot peaks are hardly B-grade. Talk to any of the awestruck travelers that mountain bike New Zealand and you get the impression that none would trade the Southern Alps for those of Hannibal and Jean-Claude.

Even with the preponderance of mountains, few countries on earth can match New Zealand's geographical diversity. Subtropical rain forests sprout less than a hundred miles from glaciers. You can depart the vast, sheep-dung-scented fields for high-country volcanoes . . . which reek of sulfur. The country's so isolated that there are no native mammals save two species of bats. Mammals would only get in the way of the many flightless birds and the cricketlike giant weta, which is the world's heaviest insect.

Geologically, the two islands differ markedly. North Island, which rides the same continental plate as India and Australia, was shaped by internal volcanic activity, and as Ruapehu recently proved, it can still blow its top. South Island is carried on the Pacific plate and isn't volcanic—although its mountains move, too. A summit slide nipped 30 feet off the top of Mount Cook a few years ago; at 12,313 feet, however, it remains the highest peak in the country.

Geologists think New Zealand once belonged to a super continent called Gondwanaland, but broke off 100 million years ago (perhaps to give Risk boards some needed symmetry). For most of those years, New Zealand was left alone. The first humans, the Maori, didn't show up until about A.D. 900. Whites came many centuries later, beginning with the Dutch navigator Tasman in 1642 and accelerating with Captain Cook in 1769.

New Zealand was the first country to let women vote (in 1893), and it remains a progressive, almost model country. Poverty is almost nonexistent and crime is low. Give the Kiwis

---

AT A GLANCE

TRIP LENGTH 14 days	PRICE RANGE (INDEPENDENT TRIP) $600
PHYSICAL CHALLENGE 1 2 ③ 4 5	PRICE RANGE (OUTFITTED GROUP TRIP) $1,300
MENTAL CHALLENGE 1 ② 3 4 5	STAGING CITY Wellington, New Zealand
PRIME TIME November–April	HEADS UP: The west side of South Island is extremely wet

Top: Sunshine Bay ride, Queenstown, South Island.
Above: Lake Wanaka and the Southern Alps in the background,
South Island.

credit. Making an advanced industrialized nation out of a couple of islands stranded 1,200 miles from their nearest neighbor takes great pluck. No question they've succeeded, and have since been able to turn their considerable talents to recreation.

Kiwi mountain biking—while not as popular as Kiwi hiking, kayaking, skiing, or bungee jumping—is superb. Riders compare it to riding California—in 1915, when only three million people lived there and you could still drink from mountain streams. As one mtb website respondent put it, "You'll have mountains as spectacular as the Sierras, but with an emerald lake in front of each one and waterfalls cascading down every slope." New Zealand is so well landscaped

it boasts more than 150 species of fern. As writer David Quammen once described the flora, "You can find yourself mesmerized by the starburst exuberance of all those chartreuse umbrellas scattered through the deeper green forest."

The national passion for hiking (or "tramping" as the Kiwis call it) has laced the mountainsides with thousands of miles of marked tracks—and most allow mountain biking. Plus, there's an efficient network of trampers' huts (many supplied by helicopter), making backcountry excursions viable for almost all riders. Wilderness travel in New Zealand means never having to carry a tent or mattress: Just ride from hut to well-stocked hut. For less than $18 per night, you get a real bed, a roof over your head, gas cooking rings, a lively social life, sinks, and sometimes flush toilets.

What's more, Kiwi riders are now building specific "mountain bike parks" such as the Makara Peak Mountain Bike Park near Karori on North Island. In America, where trail users fight constantly, a dedicated mtb park sounds like a fantasy that could never get off the ground. But Kiwis take after native son Sir Edmund Hillary: They don't seem to see the obstacles, just the goals. Says Bill Heath, an esteemed adventure sports filmmaker, "Being outside is crucial to a Kiwi. They really like to try new things. They're into going out in bad weather and doing just about anything. Kiwis are some of the least competitive but most adventurous people I've ever met."

On their return from New Zealand, pilgrims can and will expound on a number of subjects and curiosities. Eventually, though, all discussions funnel down to the same topic. Every conversational highway behaves like the proverbial road to Rome. Sooner or later, with eloquence or mumbles, the New Zealand pilgrim wants to talk about beauty.

They can't help it. Compared to New Zealand, Lake Tahoe resembles a Rust Belt slag

Windswept trees at Slope Point, South Island. New Zealand sits in the "roaring forties" latitude, which means strong winds blow from the west.

heap. Nowhere else on a mountain biker's earth does one ride mesmerizing alpine slopes poised thousands of feet above emerald fields and glacial blue lakes. Riders will compare it to both Hawaii and Switzerland in the same breath. Says Heath, "The thing that really blows me away about the Southern Hemisphere is that there's no aerial haze. Almost all of the industrial countries are in the Northern Hemisphere, and the particles stay up there. New Zealand is incredibly clear and bright. On a fair day, you can see 40 percent farther than you could up north. When I shoot it, it's almost a full stop brighter on film."

Awesome beauty. Oodles of singletrack. Outdoorsy people. Tangy fruit. If New Zealand wasn't stranded 10,000 miles away, you probably would have visited it already.

WHAT TO EXPECT

New Zealand sits in the South Pacific, separated from Australia by 1,200 miles and the Tasman Sea. Most international flights land first in Auckland. The national language is English, so getting around is simple.

Westland National Park. The Southern Alps trap moisture coming from the west, resulting in annual rainfall of 200 inches. The country boasts more than 150 species of ferns.

New Zealand's excellent road system makes bike touring a joy: Strongly consider bringing a pair of slick tires and a B.O.B. trailer.

Car travel (New Zealanders drive on the left) is also recommended as the roads are well posted and the distances short. Main train routes are few, though train travel is reasonably fast. To hop islands, the Interislander ferry connects Wellington on North Island to Picton on South Island.

The mountain biking scene mostly resembles America's: Active people riding designated recreation trails in unlittered places, often on public land. The shops are capable, but don't always contain high-quality rental bikes. Bring your own steed. Bookstores sell good mountain bike trail guides, and the bike shops often have good information.

You are guaranteed good riding around Queenstown, the bungee-jumping-riverboating-kayaking tourist mecca on South Island. Nelson, known as the sunniest spot in New Zealand, is another South Island hotbed of singletrack. On North Island, there are a number of mtb options—ranging from redwood-type forests to austere volcanoes. Check out both Rotorua and Wellington, the capital. If you plan on road-tripping the country, Wellington makes the perfect base.

Every little village in New Zealand has one or more "backpackers" hotels. You get a bed in a double, triple, or larger room and usually share a common bathroom, kitchen, and lounge facilities. Everything is as clean as the most expensive U.S. hotel.

Betting on weather is especially risky in New Zealand. It's a maritime climate and changes suddenly. The islands aren't wide enough to generate the heat that builds up high pressure. Basically, anything coming out of Australia wallops New Zealand. Mount Cook, the highest peak, is especially notorious for hosting clouds while the rest of the island bathes in sunlight. Lying between 34S and 47S, New Zealand sits squarely in the "roaring forties" latitude, which means a prevailing and continual wind blows over the country from west to east. North Island is generally the warmer isle. Note that on South Island, the Southern Alps act as a barrier for the moisture-laden winds from the Tasman Sea, which means the eastern portion of the island stays relatively dry, while the west receives 200 drenching inches of rain per year.

The most common complaint from tourists to New Zealand? Food. It's been said that the 86 percent Anglo population has preserved every bad British culinary tradition. According to Bill Heath, "The diets are pretty old-fashioned.

Tongariro National Park near the center of the North Island is a region of volcanic thermal activity, with vividly colored hot springs.

They're not really into vegetables there. They're into meat pies. I'm not really a big fan of Kiwi food—there's too much carcass."

For general information, contact the (New Zealand Tourism Board (800-388-5494; www.newzealandtourism.com).

LODGING

Again, it pays to look for backpackers' lodges wherever you travel in New Zealand. To learn

New Zealand's excellent, well-marked road system makes bike touring a joy.

about 240 quality-graded lodges, check out www.backpack.co.nz.

In the adventure mecca of Queenstown, you can flop inexpensively at the Queenstown Hostel (64-3-442-8413).

In Nelson, the Leisure Lodge Motor Inn (64-3-548-2089; Stay@LeisureLodge.co.nz) is

located near the city center and a 10-minute drive from the beach.

THE RIDES

NORTH ISLAND

Near Wellington, the Makara Peak MTB Park features several memorable trails. Among the best are Deliverance, which zigzags through supplejack vines, over roots, down streambeds, and along ridge tops, and Ridgeline, a bombing downhill singletrack with several steep bits. From the park's 1,351-foot Makara Peak are excellent views of Wellington, Cook Strait, South Island, Mana and Kapiti Island.

Big Rock Mountain Bike Park, located two hours south of Auckland near Tokoroa, contains 18 miles of trail in a landscape mixing pine forest and volcanic ash. Big Rock's seven loops contain lots of singletrack and technical challenges.

SOUTH ISLAND

The Queen Charlotte Walkway is a premier three- or four-day jaunt that covers 57 miles—42 of them singletrack! It begins in Ships Cove, then traces the ridges above the Marlborough Sounds to Anikiwa. Porters will take your luggage from hotel to hotel while you pedal above forest- and beach-studded panoramas.

Skippers Canyon, located 17 miles from Queenstown in the Southern Lakes Region, is a singletrack haven where trails are perched on cliffsides hundreds of yards above the raging Shotover River. The terrain mixes austere, sepia-toned bush regions with forested canyons.

OUFITTERS AND BIKE SHOPS

Planet Bike is an imaginative outfit that offers heli biking, night rides, and mostly singletrack in Whakarewarewa Forest where the huge trees evoke redwoods. Planet Bike is based on North Island, near Rotorua and its belching volcanoes.

Mud Cycles is a progressive shop in Wellington: It hosts trail maintenance parties, runs races,

Cairn on Queenstown Hill, the Southern Alps.

and jokes that it's the "best bike shop in the known universe." One of New Zealand's capitals of mtb culture.

Operating out of Christchurch on South Island, Mainland Mountain Bike Adventures takes customers to pine-forest singletrack, high-altitude climbs, and scorching downhills.

Natural High Adrenalin Dealers is a shop as well as an outfitter in sunny Nelson (on South Island).

PLANET BIKE
30 Clouston Crescent
Rotorua, New Zealand
64-7-348-9971
www.planetbike.co.nz
$200 for 2 days

MUD CYCLES
1 Allington Road
Wellington, New Zealand
64-4-476-4961
www.mudcycles.co.nz

MAINLAND MOUNTAIN BIKE ADVENTURES
11 Nirvana St,
Brooklands, Christchurch, New Zealand
64-3-329-8747
www.mountainbiketours.co.nz
$70 per day

NATURAL HIGH ADRENALIN DEALERS
52 Rutherford Street.
Nelson, New Zealand
64-3-546-6936
www.natural-high.co.nz/
$70 per day

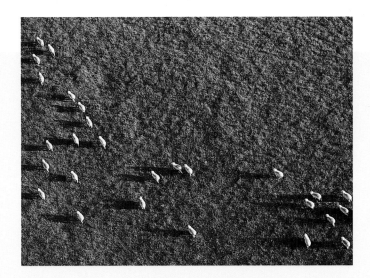

COUNTING SHEEP

Wherever you ride in New Zealand, you'll see fleece-coated domestic livestock. Sheep in New Zealand provide wool, mutton, and widespread numeric bewilderment: No one seems to know just how many sheep there are, and a qualified sheep census is clearly mandated. You'll hear estimates anywhere between 50 and 80 million, which are invariably accompanied by their ratio to humans. These are overwhelming numbers—15:1 or 25:1 or whatever—and would be terrifying to Kiwis in the unlikely event that sheep develop opposable thumbs or any semblance of brains. But until that happens, sheep merely chew their cud and lend New Zealand a pastoral, rustic air. At any rate, New Zealand is the world's biggest producer of mutton and lamb and the second-largest exporter of wool. As a result, gift shops stock every imaginable kind of sheep doll—sheep on mountain bikes, sheep in ski suits, sheep wearing Oakleys.

RECOMMENDED READING

■ *LONELY PLANET: NEW ZEALAND* (2000. $17.95. Lonely Planet.) A fine general guidebook.
■ As for mtb guidebooks, get *CLASSIC NEW ZEALAND MOUNTAIN BIKE RIDES,* by well-known Kiwi riders Paul, Simon, and Jonathan Kennett. (1999. $20.95. Kennett Bros.) Covers 400 rides from Cape Reinga to Scott Base.

■ *THE BONE PEOPLE,* Keri Hulme (1986. $13.95. Viking Press.) A provocative fable about three fiercely unique and spiritually adrift characters, that weaves its story together with dreams, myths and legends, the world of the dead, and the ways of ancient Maori cultures.

At dawn, an ash plume drifts over Mount Ngauruhoe, June 1996. Mount Ruapehu had just erupted.

Tsali & Pisgah National Forest

Botanists call this chunk of Appalachia temperate rain forest.
The mtb translation: Dust is rare; traction is great.

While riding one humid summer day in the Great Smoky Mountains of western North Carolina, I swore I could feel my whiskers growing. Why not? Everything else in the forest seemed to be sprouting with haste. Rhododendrons and flame azaleas threw vines over any stationary matter. Trees shot hundreds of feet into the sky. A mist rose from the damp, mushroom-strewn forest floor. It felt like I was riding inside a terrarium.

Western North Carolina blooms with so many trees that the state actually dedicated a memorial forest to Joyce Kilmer, the poet who wrote, "I think that I shall never see/a poem lovely as a tree"—even though Kilmer isn't from North Carolina and "Trees" is kind of a cheesy poem. Well if anything's more flowery than lame poetry, it's the flora of the Smokies. You can describe it with words that nobody ever heard of 20 years ago, like "bio-diverse." Or you can start

Great Smoky Mountains, North Carolina, earning their name.

naming the local trees—the ash, basswood, beech, birch, box elder, buckeye, butternut—and wear out before you even get to those that begin with the letter "c." There are tropical-looking trees and alpine-looking trees, new trees growing out of dead trees. Fact: You can see more arboreal species while walking the 75 or so miles across the Smokies than you would walking from London to Moscow.

This neck of the Appalachians contains 6,684-foot Mount Mitchell and several more of the biggest peaks east of the Mississippi. Yet on these lofty summits, you rarely see rocky precipices, jutting crags, or any naked ribs of earth. All you see is floor-to-ceiling forest. Happily, mountain bikers have found that these dense forests cloak hundreds (if not thousands) of miles of trails.

Most western North Carolina riders land first in Asheville, a shady city where the rich and famous gathered to "take the mountain air" back in the 1920s. Asheville's breezy plateau once hosted ritzy tuberculosis sanitariums; now it holds liberal arts colleges and Dia-Compe, a mountain bike component company. The latter tests its products in the surrounding Pisgah National Forest, where riding all the available trail combinations could take a month. The trails range from shorties like Spencer Branch, where an Asheville businesswoman could taste a couple creek crossings on her lunch break, to Laurel Mountain Trail, a multi-hour test piece littered with unmoveable boulders, huge log waterbars, and hairy switchbacks.

With 50 inches of rain per year, Pisgah's trails tend to be wet, rocky, rooty, and fairly technical. Inexperienced riders may not love them, but dirtheads will revel in them. The woods shorten horizons, making every bend in the trail a mystery. This, and Pisgah's terrain challenges, render boredom impossible.

Moving west from Pisgah, riders enter another majestic national forest, the Nantahala. Named after the Cherokee word for "Land of the Noon Day Sun," it reflects the fact that the sun penetrates to the bottom of the magnificent Nantahala River Gorge only in the middle of the day.

The ever-green Nantahala, which sits just south of Great Smoky Mountains National Park, demands to be traveled. For one, there's the scenery of the Smokies: a sea of flowing curves topped by a dreamy blue haze that reaches all the way up to heaven. For two, there's the Nantahala Outdoor Center (NOC).

A bike shop/outfitter that draws more than

AT A GLANCE

TRIP LENGTH 6 days	PRICE RANGE (INDEPENDENT TRIP) $300
PHYSICAL CHALLENGE 1 2 ③ 4 5	PRICE RANGE (OUTFITTED GROUP TRIP) $650
MENTAL CHALLENGE 1 ② 3 4 5	STAGING CITY Asheville, North Carolina
PRIME TIME Spring and fall	HEADS UP Pisgah National Forest trails are significantly rockier than those in the Tsali

Autumn, which lasts nearly four months in the Great Smokies, is tops for biking.

1,000 riders to its mtb races, NOC is actually better known for its world-class whitewater. America's canoeing and kayaking Olympians train there. Walk around the NOC and marvel as kayakers with rippling upper bodies and withered legs commingle with pigeon-chested mountain bikers with burgeoning quads. The net result is a concentration of recreation junkies that's remarkable even by Colorado or California standards. It's a revelation to see it here in southern Appalachia, a region that may never live down *Deliverance* and its stereotypes of loutish rednecks and creepy hillbillies. Experiencing the NOC—say, with a black bean soup at its riverside restaurant—makes visitors discard their silly biases and gain a pure appreciation of the South's lush beauty.

And NOC sits just a short jaunt from the Nantahala National Forest's acclaimed Tsali Recreation Area. Tsali ("SAH-lee") is located only 50 miles west of Asheville, yet its paths differ dramatically from those in the Pisgahs. Indeed, they're regarded as some of the smoothest, best-contoured trails in existence.

Tsali is a wooded sanctuary situated on a peninsula sticking out into breathtaking Lake Fontana. Tsali boasts velvety, uncluttered trails because it lies in the rain shadow of the Nantahala Mountains. Compared to other parts of North Carolina, which are normally about as dry as a toga party at Caligula's, Tsali is little damaged by liquid. It sees none of the big gullywasher rains that roll rocks and debris down trails in the Pisgah.

Opposite: Lone rider, Cane Creek, North Carolina, near Asheville.

North Carolina offers a range of trails, from relatively easy rides in Nantahala National Forest to up-and-down technical singletrack in Pisgah.

the main Tsali trailhead accesses more than 40 exhilarating miles of singletrack.

Botanists call the western North Carolina portion of Appalachia temperate rain forest. The mtb translation: Dust is rare, traction is great. On climbs, it can seem literally impossible to spin out your back wheel. On descents, you'll feel confident to step on the gas. If you're feeling good, take advantage of Tsali's smoothness by soaring off its rounded, earthen waterbars. After all, it's natural to pitch yourself into the wild blue yonder in North Carolina—home to the Wright brothers' first plane flights and birthplace of Michael "Air" Jordan. Just don't land in a tree.

WHAT TO EXPECT

The ideal gateway city is Asheville, a pretty city of tall trees and grand homes. But Atlanta, which may offer cheaper airfares, is only four hours away.

Western North Carolina boasts four-season riding, although the winters have many wet and cold days. Summer in the Smokies is hot (with daytime temperatures in the 80s) but not at all unpleasant. Spring, meanwhile, brings such a profusion of alpine iris and other wildflowers that only a tiny ribbon of trail is visible through the blooms. Because elevations in the Smokies range dramatically, from 800 to 6,600 feet, peak springtime lasts from March to June depending on the altitude. Autumn is the same way. And the fall foliage is spectacular.

The stunning vegetational variety of western North Carolina includes wild blackberries. Pick the plumpest and enjoy, but keep your eye open for charismatic megafauna: Black bears dig those berries, too.

Most of the rides take place in the Pisgah and Nantahala National Forests. The Pisgah, which surrounds Asheville, is known for technical riding and big elevation changes (especially on Laurel and Buckhorn trails). The Nantahala

In Tsali, you can shift to the middle ring and just fly. The nicely packed dirt climbs plenty of hills, but none are too big or too steep. You negotiate some switchbacks into leafy ravines and take some time at the overlooks to gaze at the Disneyland-blue waters of Lake Fontana, but mostly you cruise so fast and so effortlessly that it's seriously difficult to suppress giggles. Oh, and

Opposite: Experienced riders thrive on Pisgah's trails, which tend to be wet, rocky, rooty, and technical.

contains smoother, less steep trails that will make intermediates feel like experts and experts feel like gods. These are highlighted by the loops at Tsali Recreation Area located just south of Great Smoky Mountains National Park near the town of Almond.

No matter what ride you choose, you'll pedal in dark forests. If myopia or simple good sense dictates that you ride with eyewear, consider replacing dark lenses with orange or yellow ones.

For general information, contact North Carolina Tourism (800 VISIT NC; email: inquiry@travel.commerce.state.nc.us; www-commerce. state.nc.us/tourism).

LODGING

Five thousand feet up the slopes of Mount Pisgah sits the woodsy Pisgah Inn (828-235-8228; email: PisgahInn@aol.com). Open only during the warmer months, its private porches look out over fragrant balsams, mist-filled coves, and tall peaks.

Nantahala Village (704-488-9616) lies just a few miles from Tsali and it welcomes mountain bikers: Its property has hosted races, it serves good food in big portions, and boasts spacious rooms for all your gear.

The Tsali Recreation Area Campground (704-479-6431) allows you to sleep right at this revered trailhead. The $15 fee covers flush toilets, hot showers, bike wash, and beachfront access to the swimming in Lake Fontana.

THE RIDES

TSALI

Combining Tsali's Left Loop and Right Loop creates a 20-odd-mile wonder that fast riders can complete in three housrs. You're riding singletrack the whole way—whipping through green tunnels, cornering into the umpteen coves that riddle the Lake Fontana shoreline—but moving at fire road speeds, which is nothing less than a turbocharged kick in the pants. One caveat: Bikes and horses share a rotating trail use schedule at Tsali, meaning Left and Right loops are open for mtb use only Mondays, Wednesdays, Fridays, and Sundays. On the other days, ride Tsali's shorter (but still excellent) Thompson and Mouse Branch loops.

PISGAH

Wilson Ridge Trail is a 15-mile out-and-back located in the Pisgah National Forest near the town of Blowing Rock. It's a beautifully forested and highly technical singletrack that climbs more than 2,000 feet. The return descent is a brake-frying blast. Call 704-652-2144 for more info.

Staire Creek is something like a theme park ride. This Pisgah ride skirts enormous trees, a huge cliff face, a rocky cave, and a waterfall. Plus, it has a thrilling downhill singletrack that drops 1,200 feet in less than a mile.

OUTFITTERS AND BIKE SHOPS

The Nantahala Outdoor Center offers a variety of mountain bike programs, including single-

THE ORIGINAL CAROLINA TAR HEELS

North Carolina was christened in honor of King Charles I of England. Its choice of nickname, the Tar Heel State, seems a little odd, since "tar heel" was an insulting name applied to the state's infantrymen during the Civil War by Mississippi soldiers who complained that the men from North Carolina didn't hold their positions—that is, they didn't put "tar on their heels."

track camps, women's camps, wildflower weekends, and fall color weekends. It rents high-quality bikes, and its mechanics are the best equipped in the Nantahala National Forest.

In Asheville, your mechanical needs can be met by Hearn's Cycling and Fitness.

NANTAHALA OUTDOOR CENTER
13077 Highway 19 West
Bryson City, NC 28713
828-488-2175
www.noc.com
$85 per day

HEARN'S CYCLING AND FITNESS
34 Broadway
Asheville, NC 28801
828-253-4800

RECOMMENDED READING
The two best guidebooks are both from Jim Parham's Off the Beaten Track series:
■ *A GUIDE TO MOUNTAIN BIKING IN WESTERN NORTH CAROLINA* (1992. $12.95. WMC Publishing.) *MOUNTAIN BIKING IN PISGAH NATIONAL FOREST* (1992. $12.95. WMC Publishing.) Volume I covers the Smokies, including Nantahala National Forest, and Volume II covers Pisgah National Forest.
■ *OUR SOUTHERN HIGHLANDERS*, Horace Kephart (1977. $16.95. University of Tennessee Press.) Written in 1913, this compelling, nonfiction look at the early hillbillies living in Carolina's overgrown, inaccessible mountains is the first and still the most illuminating book to chronicle the harsh lives and amazing pluck of those people "enmeshed in a mountain labyrinth that has deflected and repelled the march of our nation." Mountain bikers will especially appreciate Kephart's fascination with the severe tilt of the Smokies.

Tsali's Left Loop and Right Loop create a 20-mile singletrack ride through green tunnels along Lake Fontana's shoreline.

Cape Town, the Garden Route & Johannesburg

Trails are opening up all over "the Beloved Country."
Some are game paths that in the previous six decades
saw only deer and the occasional poacher.

R obbie Powell, a white mountain biker, frequently bookends his backcountry excursions with visits to *shebeens*, the quasi-legal bars where blacks in South Africa's townships drink. Because the 1994 end of apartheid failed to erase all the country's racial tension, many of Powell's Causcasian friends think he's daft to mix with blacks on their sometimes hostile turf. But Powell responds, "Hey, I'm as African as they are."

As South Africa warms to concepts such as integration, South Africans will follow Powell's example. But one can't blame anyone for questioning how to behave in the recently remade South Africa. Sure, the area has been developed since Portuguese sailors rounded the Cape of Good Hope in 1488. But for all intents and purposes, "The Beloved Country" is a new one, full of strange opportunities and unopened gifts.

Powell, at least, has explored terra incognito

World-famous mtb stunt-meister Hans Rey pulls a wheelie on the Cape Town cliffs.

before. As much as anyone, he brought the odd universe of mountain biking to South Africa. He broke into biking in 1989, back when there were so few riders on South Africa's velds and mountains that "you could tell who was out by their tire tracks." After pioneering routes on the country's southern tip, he formed an outfitter operation called Outeniqua Biking Trails and helped found the South Africa Mountain Bike Association.

Now Powell is delving deep into both the culture and the landscapes of post-apartheid South Africa. Certainly, this is a grand time to do so, as South Africa brims with optimism and bonhomie like it never has before. Blacks are exhilarated over freedom gained, whites feel a dazed relief that a hateful system is gone—and mountain bikers are riding places they never could a few years earlier. Why? Because during apartheid, the national forests were all but kept as private reserves for the rich, meaning they were basically closed to all. Today's new order mandates use by the people, for the people. Trails are opening up all over; some are overgrown game paths that in the last six decades have seen only deer and the occasional poacher.

South Africa has long been recognized as one of the globe's most beautiful countries. Apartheid kept travelers away, though, so the country's matchless scenery and wildlife are untouched by the ravages of tourism. Now mountain bikers are plying the high plateaus, chains of tall mountains, and dramatic coastline here at the end of the world. Everywhere they pedal, they see evidence of South Africa's magnificent flora. The country lists 22,000 different species, with wildflowers such as raging red hot pokers in the grasslands, weird succulents blooming after spring rains, and one of the world's six recognized floral kingdoms—botanists call it the Cape kingdom—beautifying the southwest. Large areas in the north are covered by a savannah-type vegetation, characterized by acacias and thorn trees, while the southern coast accounts for much of South Africa's forest—exotic mixes of fern, lemonwood, and giant yellowwood.

South Africa's national parks, reserves, and botanical gardens are among the best-managed conservation areas in the world—and many allow mountain biking. Perhaps Kenya and Tanzania became more famous for wildlife during apartheid. Yet South Africa best delivers one's mind's-eye vision of the Dark Continent. When it comes to land mammals, South Africa

AT A GLANCE

TRIP LENGTH 11 days	PRICE RANGE (INDEPENDENT TRIP) $500
PHYSICAL CHALLENGE 1 2 ③ 4 5	PRICE RANGE (OUTFITTED GROUP TRIP) $1,400
MENTAL CHALLENGE 1 2 ③ 4 5	STAGING CITY Cape Town, South Africa
PRIME TIME April–November	HEADS UP Johannesburg is notorious for its rape problem and other crime

In the new South Africa, blacks are exhilarated over freedom gained, whites are relieved that apartheid is gone—and mountain bikers are riding places they never could a few years ago.

hogs the superlatives: it's got the biggest (the African elephant), the smallest (the pygmy shrew), the tallest (the giraffe) and the fastest (the cheetah). The country also contains the last substantial populations of black and white rhinos—with horns intact. South Africa's benevolent climate warms the nests of the ostrich (the world's largest bird) and the Kori bustard (the largest flying bird). Crocodiles lurk and hippos rampage in its streams and rivers. Elephants and zebras enjoy their own dedicated reserves.

After mountain biking South Africa a couple years ago, Michael DiGregorio returned home to Los Angeles with tales of being hassled by baboons. "To their point of view, you're a dangerous, fast-moving burst of artificially bright colors. They might swipe at you if you don't make eye contact with them. I once found myself surrounded by baboons that mimicked Oakland Raider fans, arrogantly pulling back lips to expose a snarl and flashing blunt, daggerlike canines."

Like Powell and most local riders, DiGregorio is white. Blacks rarely mountain bike because they can't afford it. They remain poor (earning but 29 percent of the income of South Africa while comprising 76 percent of the population), and can hardly be blamed for resenting the affluence whites built during apartheid. A typical white home contains imposing gates, a large garden, and a swimming pool, and most whites enjoy a standard of living and way of life comparable to

Opposite:Harkerville Forest's easy grades and variety make for some of the finest cycling in the country.

people in the world's most developed countries. They're well-off people with leisure time—in other words, the same kind who built and still support mountain biking in North America. And so it goes in South Africa. While blacks and ethnic Asians struggle with unemployment, affluent whites may be blowing off work to carve the exquisite singletracks through the Cape of Good Hope's verdant wine country or among the sheer, 3,000-foot escarpments in the Drakensberg Mountains, South Africa's highest.

Fortunately, the infant tourism industry is playing something of an economic equalizer. Unlike South Africa's old mainstay—the gold industry—tourism puts income in a variety of pockets and provides thousands of decent jobs. With the demise of apartheid, tourism is increasing by as much as 50 percent a year. We should all like to contribute to such increases, for South Africa deserves a visit on its mtb merits alone. The fact that it's one of the world's most exciting, intriguing, and gorgeous countries is just icing on the cake—presumably, a cake that treats both vanilla and chocolate with dignity.

WHAT TO EXPECT

One of the 20 largest nations on Earth, South Africa anchors the Dark Continent and separates the Atlantic from the Indian Ocean deep in the Southern Hemisphere. English, one of the nation's official languages, will serve you well in most cases. Know that there are 11 main tribal languages as well: If you attempt even a few Zulu words and phrases, it'll be appreciated.

Most tourists gravitate eventually to Cape Town, South Africa's oldest settlement and an unequivocally gorgeous city. Its mountains—dominated by the kilometer-high flat-topped Table Mountain—offer outrageous views of the crashing Atlantic. Vineyards, beaches, and singletracks sit within easy reach. Another prime area for riding mirrors the "Garden Route," the prim, British name for the beautiful coastline along the southwest coast. The Garden Route has some of the most significant tracts of indigenous forest in the country, and many prime rides. Knysna, a bohemian Garden Route town on the Indian Ocean beach, offers a high-tech bike shop, accesses several classic rides, and generally serves as

DEATH BY HIPPO

Of all the quintessentially African species padding around the veldt and forests of South Africa, the most dangerous to humans is the common (but still quite strange) hippopotamus. Heavy-bodied, short-legged, and characterized by the tiny eyes and ears on top of its big head, the hippo has always seemed cartoonish, and therefore cuddly. But no—these hoofed mammals with pointed incisors and canine teeth kill more people than South Africa's crocodiles and big cats combined. Hippos, which are semiaquatic and can stay underwater for as long as 25 minutes, often seem to object to humans boating their rivers. Like their counterparts in large mammaldom, the elephants, old bull hippos sometimes channel their 9,000 pounds into murder mode for little reason at all. Perhaps it has something to do with the fact that hippos are still hunted: South Africans shoot them with harpoons or chase them into hidden pits, all because hippos sport edible meat and their hides make a nice soup. At any rate, these piglike animals that can swim 20 miles a day and sometimes go by the name "river horses" aren't disclosing their mysteries. For instance, science still doesn't know why fossils of the same species as the present-day hippo have turned up in chilly England. Here's a guess—the ever-weird *Hippopotamus amphibius* was called there by sonar signals from Stonehenge.

Mtb areas near Cape Town offer stunning views of the city plus switchbacks, rocky descents, and oddly angled roots.

South Africa's mtb capital. Johannesburg and the Drakensberg Mountains feature several good rides in eastern South Africa, but if time's short, you may want to forsake these eastern destinations for the southwest.

Mountain biking still ranks well below water sports and soccer in South Africa, but the generally sporty populace is embracing it. And there are almost no trail access conflicts. Still, it's a long way from Durango. Riders are still waiting for an mtb-specific guidebook, and it can be tough to rent a top-flight full-suspension bike. Bring your own bike or prepare to ride a hardtail.

Hardtails, incidentally, work just fine here, as trails tend to contain large segments of forgiving dirt. Higher elevation areas may contain clusters of fist-sized rocks, while lower elevation rides can be muddy and boggy. But in general, animals—especially baboons—present the most formidable trail hazards. Snakes do occupy much of the country.

Its position just south of the Tropic of Capricorn makes South Africa a mostly dry and sunny place but the climate is moderated by its topography and the surrounding oceans. The east tends to be wetter and more tropical than the west, though Cape Town gets its share of rain. Winters are mild everywhere except in the highest country, where there are frosts and occasional snowfalls. Bring wet-weather gear and you should be happy.

For official South African tourism information, contact the embassy in Washington (202-232-4400) or www.southafrica.net.

LODGING

In Witelsbos (near Knysna) are the log cabins of Nigel and Lizette Lok (27-42-750-3816; email:

Top: Beach huts at False Bay, Cape Town.
Above: Mtb race on Table Mountain.

is the ideal location for recreational mountain biking. The relatively easy gradients and diversity of the rides offer some of the finest cycling in the Southern Cape. The name of the trailhead—Garden of Eden—indicates the region's beauty. Indeed, one of Harkerville's four loops passes by a small glade of coast redwood, which was imported from California and planted in 1927. Another loop contains a shady swimming hole, while yet another has been called the "best ride in the Southern Hemisphere" for its twisty forest singletrack and breathtaking cliffside exposures.

In the Northwest Province, the Dome Highland mtb trails are situated in the Vredefort Dome, one of earth's largest meteorite impact sites. A 1,308-yard meteorite parked itself here almost 200 million years ago: Try not to emulate it during the ride's technical challenges and fast downhills.

Tokai Manorhouse, which begins just outside of Cape Town, offers a downhiller-friendly recipe of riding: a winding, moderately steep gravel road uphill, followed with a fast and technical singletrack downhill. All told, it's a 13-mile ride. Lush forests and plentiful baboons add to the scenery.

Also near Cape Town is the Stellenbosch mtb area, which has hosted World Cup competitions. Proffering off-camber switchbacks, rocky descents, oddly angled roots—and trail names like Snake Pit and Fat Boys Jump—Stellenbosch is tricky, challenging, and fun.

Near Johannesburg at the CR Swart Dam area is a technical ride called Sweat and Gears: It's an all-singletrack network, riddled with steep pitches, jumps, deep forest, sand, dust, and logs.

OUTFITTERS AND BIKE SHOPS

Outeniqua Biking Trails escorts riders through the Garden Route's lush forests and sweet-tasting streams, and up to the spectacular heights of the Outeniqua Mountains. Plus, the outfit houses riders in fully equipped cabins in the heart of the

bookings@tsitsikamma.co.za). The cabins are located in a fern-dotted gorge alongside a river and make a nice, tranquil base for exploring the Harkerville Forest.

Along the Garden Route, the Lyngrove Country House (27-21-842-2116) is a luxurious lodge located near False Bay. Recreate on the surrounding mtb trails or in the vineyards that encircle Lyngrove.

If you're riding the Stellenbosch trials, you might want to camp at the Algeria Forest Station (27-02-682-3440), where the leafy woods draw much praise and the RVs can be escaped.

THE RIDES

Situated along the Garden Route between Knysna and Plettenberg Bay, Harkerville Forest

Buffelsnek indigenous forest.

AFTRAC, an outfitter in the Johannesburg region, organizes night rides, mtb safaris, races, and other events.

Knysna Cycle Works was recently sold by Robbie Powell to a group that includes a mechanic who graduated from cycling's prestigious Barnett Institute in Colorado. Knysna Cycle Works can definitely point you to the area's best trails: Staffers have built some of them.

Near Johannesburg, seek out Morningside Cycles. It can meet most service needs and it offers group rides for any and all.

Homestead boys, Bo Kaap (Malay Quarter) Cape Town.

OUTENIQUA BIKING TRAILS
P.O. Box 2
Harkerville, 6604 South Africa
27-44-532-7644
Email: info@gardenroute.co.za
www.gardenroute.co.za/plett/obt/main.htm
$875 for 3 days

AFTRAC
P.O. Box 1059
Olivedale, 2158, Gauteng, South Africa
27-11-79-41713
www.home.global.co.za/~aftrac
Cost: $350 for 4 days

KNYSNA CYCLE WORKS
PO Box 2658
Kynsna, 6570, South Africa
27-44-382-5153
www.cycle.gardenroute.co.za

MORNINGSIDE CYCLES
27-11-784-2154
Email: Dentonb@smcsoft.co.za

RECOMMENDED READING
■ Lonely Planet's guidebook, SOUTH AFRICA, LESOTHO & SWAZILAND (2000. $17.95. Lonely Planet.) covers the mean streets of Johannesburg, the produce in picturesque South African vineyards, the wildlife-rich national parks, and more.

■ As of early 2000, South African mountain biking lacked a detailed off-road guidebook. For more general info, including some trail reports, see BICYCLING IN AFRICA, David Mozer (1993. $14.00. Intl. Bicycle Fund.)

■ SOUTH FROM THE LIMPOPO: TRAVELS THROUGH SOUTH AFRICA, Dervla Murphy (1999. $26.05. Overlook Press.) Describes the author's quest to take South Africa's pulse from 1993 (during the violence preceding Nelson Mandela's election) through 1995 (when the Beloved Country's assorted wounds began to heal). Murphy achieves this by riding her bike some 6,000 miles, pedaling gnarly terrain and dealing with hostile peoples of every color.

The Alps

In a nation where 70 percent of the terrain is mountainous, all-terrain bikes are exploring heights previously known only to demons and grazing cows.

In the ancient Swiss village of Champéry, where pitched roofs lean so far over narrow streets that they almost block the views of the massive Alps, you savor your preamble to the ride. As you step out of your quaint, family-owned hotel, the doughy perfume of a bakery fills your nostrils. You roll by a brasserie and a small sports shop, turn left at an alleyway, pass a shed that's older than any country in the New World, cross a yard where a solitary cow munches cud,

and board a huge tram up to the vast Portes du Soleil ski area—where 23 lifts (operating from June until September) deliver you to tight technical descents, rolling dirt roads, or meandering, high-altitude trails that take you from Switzerland to France and back.

Near Lake Lucerne, you climb up a creek that drains pure glacial waters into the fjordlike arms of the lake to the Crazy Monk Trail. There you'll learn of the dragons, witches, and demons

No other mtb destination can match the Swiss Alps' developed trail networks and immense vertical drops.

that were said to inhabit the mountains' raw upper slopes. Then, whether scary monsters give chase or not, you can bomb like a crazy monk down a 3,000-vertical-foot downhill singletrack.

In Château d'Oex, a small dairy and tourist village nestled in a lush green valley just east of Lake Geneva, you attempt the "gnarly" downhill course that bruised elite racers at the 1997 World Championships. Surf the huge slalom-style turns, navigate the narrow chutes between rocks, rail the tight slippery singletrack through the trees, survive the steep switchbacks, and splash across the creek that served as the finish line. Then, wish you did it all during the '97 Worlds, when the finish area was manned by local farmers selling fresh milkshakes and L'Etivaz cheese.

From Zermatt—a charming Alpine village that honors the natural magnificence surrounding the 14,687-foot Matterhorn by forbidding automobile traffic—you undertake the ultimate in mtb hedonism. You take a series of cable cars, trams, and trains to ascend mountains, then coast gloriously down all day—stopping only to fuel up on cheese, chocolate, Euro coffee, and wine. The terrain varies from glorious, *Sound of Music*-type meadows to cobblestone staircases in tidy village squares.

Clearly, Switzerland has embraced the mountain bike with all the passion its Teutonic heart can master. Here, where 70 percent of the terrain is mountainous, all-terrain bikes are exploring heights previously known only to demons and grazing cows. It seems like common sense. Yet just a few years ago, Switzerland's prim tourist offices knew much more about cuckoo clocks than mtb trails. Not anymore. Now the famously brainy Swiss (who have won more Nobel Prizes and registered more patents per capita than any other nation on earth) are using their intellect to explore the vast potential of mountain biking the Alps.

The Swiss have diligently catalogued their wealth of hiking trails, farm access roads, and forested footpaths. They've erected great numbers of mtb-specific signposts. They've opened their grand, glacier-top huts to multi-day mtb tours. They've turned their immense ski resort infrastructure into a summer service for mountain bikers. While Goethe prefigured mountain biking by quite a few decades, his pithy description of Switzerland still applies: This off-road fantasyland is still a combination of "the colossal

Overleaf: Racing downhill at the 1997 World Championships, Château d'Oex.

AT A GLANCE

TRIP LENGTH 10 days	**PRICE RANGE (INDEPENDENT TRIP)** $700
PHYSICAL CHALLENGE 1 2 3 4 ⑤	**PRICE RANGE (OUTFITTED GROUP TRIP)** $1,400
MENTAL CHALLENGE 1 ② 3 4 5	**STAGING CITY** Geneva, Switzerland
PRIME TIME June–September	**HEADS UP** Many restaurants frown on dirty, tattered bike clothes

and the well-ordered."

Of course, riders seeking to "get away from it all" don't necessarily want signs at every trail bend. Nor do they savor the constant presence of hikers and other tourists—not to mention the concomitant high prices. Sure, life in the Swiss Alps is reliably clean, safe, and efficient. But the Swiss passion for order and tidiness can be a bit unnerving: It's "coziness under strict control," as a traveler quoted in *Lonely Planet Switzerland* described it.

Somehow, Switzerland's disparate people have developed a singular mind against despoiling the Alps. The country encompasses four cultures: French (Geneva and the surrounding western area), Italian (Lugano and the surrounding southern area), Swiss-German (Zurich and the surrounding eastern area), and Romansh (St. Moritz and the surrounding southeastern region). The French and Italian areas are considered more lively and cosmopolitan and the Romansh and German areas more conservative and sedate. Whatever. It's all Europe. Which means not just crowds and linguistic collisions, but nice things, like elaborate gardens and mountain lookout restaurants that have absolutely zero taboos governing beer or wine.

The Swiss Alps can represent Europe at its most elitist, but they're still a kick to pedal. You base your rides from towns lined with gorgeous wooden chalets and restaurants adorned with terraces, umbrellas, and flower boxes spilling over with geraniums. You fill your pack with baguettes and cheese at the quaint local market, then point your wheel along sparkling streets where the views down the valley resemble the landscapes on a chocolate box.

Keeping an eye on the great gray ridges and ancient glaciers, you enter proud conifer forests (which, incidentally, cover a quarter of Switzerland). You spin and spin up above timberline to alpine meadows. Above the cows, you try (and fail) to match the speed and agility of mountain animals: the ibex (a mountain goat with huge curved horns) and the chamois (a horned antelope whose soft hide is made into cloths for cleaning cars).

When you finish climbing, take a while to catch your breath. You'll need it, for no other mtb destination on the globe can match the Swiss Alps' blend of developed trail networks and gargantuan vertical drops. The downhills define Swiss mountain biking. Do they make the Alps the ultimate place to pedal? Well, the area's profusion of scrub, rocks, cows, and tourists may never allow the Zenlike aesthetics of singletrack riding in the remote American West. On the other hand, such huge, long, crazy descents simply do not exist back home, and, indeed, are difficult for a North American even to conceive. Adrenaline junkies and gravity hogs will no doubt respond appropriately. Which is to say that, when bombing down an mtb trail in the Swiss Alps, it's sometimes hard to determine whether the source of all that screaming is the brakes or you.

WHAT TO EXPECT

Switzerland sits squarely in the gut of western Europe, landlocked by France, Germany, Liechtenstein, Austria, and Italy. The Alps occupy the

Above: The huge, long, crazy downhills define Swiss mountain biking.
Opposite: "Keeping an eye on the great gray ridges and ancient glaciers, you enter proud conifer forests…"

Top: The Matterhorn at sunset. Above: Senior men's start at the 1997 World Championships, Château d'Oex.

for extra baggage (if necessary).

Consider bringing panniers and a rack. Bicycle touring in Switzerland has been called "one of the great undiscovered pleasures of European travel." The scenery is glorious, the roads perfectly kept and superbly marked. The Swiss Alps region is small enough for you to cover a lot of ground in a short time and there are excellent maps. Everything is so well organized that you do not really need to go to the expense of a group tour. And when you don't feel like riding, trains and buses will gladly carry your bike.

Whatever you do, don't underestimate the Alps. The mountains are steep, rocky, unpredictable, and sometimes downright severe. It pays to be in good physical condition for the continuous, two-hour uphills. Bring a basic first-aid kit. Many outfitters insist you also carry emergency evacuation insurance.

Travelers need to be prepared for a range of temperatures depending on altitude. There is perennial snow cover at altitudes above 10,000 feet. Summer is the most pleasant time for outdoor pursuits. Unfortunately, you won't be the only tourist during summer, so prices can be high, accommodations hard to find, and the mainstream sights crowded. You'll find much better deals and fewer crowds in late September to October.

For an overview on the country, contact Swiss Tourism in the United States (800-GO-SWISS; 212-757-5944; www.switzerland-tourism.ch/).

LODGING

If lodging is called a "sporthotel" you know it probably tolerates the clatter of bike cleats on linoleum. Top Sporthotel Stoos (41-810-45-15; sporthotel-stoos@bluewin.ch) is a modern four-star hotel in a quiet, car-free resort village, 4,200 feet above Lake Lucerne. Good, nearby rides abound; you can probably see them from the spa.

central and southern regions of the country. Premier mtb destinations are found in both French- and German-speaking regions. The Swiss Alps aren't a vast area, but the twisty roads make fast travel difficult. You can cover all the areas listed here in a week, but it would be much more relaxing to do so in two weeks.

Mountain bikers will find the Swiss Alps very accommodating: There are well-marked trails, a great variety of rides, and highly competent shops. You can find high-quality rental bikes; just remember that the rental prices are high ($25 to $50 a day) and that it's certainly cheaper to fly one's bike packed in a box and pay

The three-star Hotel De Ville (41-26-924-74-77; www.Hotel-de-Ville.Oex@planet.ch) offers fine views of the lush valley surrounding Château d'Oex.

In Zermatt, the Hotel Slalom (41-967-19-77) has an excellent location over the river; some rooms contain private showers and TV.

Camping in Switzerland is a mixed bag: the sites are beautiful, but they're usually far from the towns. Call the Swiss Camping Association (41-033-823-35-23) for info.

THE RIDES

From Zermatt, perhaps Switzerland's most bike-crazed town, you can ride a plethora of fine trails. To do the all-day downhill described on page 165, ride along the Vispe River to St. Nicholas. Keep going past the waterfalls to Kapalltran, ride up in a cable car, climb up 600 feet, descend to Moos Alp, eat lunch, plunge down more singletracks to Visp, then catch the train back to Zermatt.

The town of Grindelwald makes a great base for exploring local trails. Try the twisting, 4,000-foot climb to the summit of Mannlichen Ridge (7,300 feet) for spectacular views over the Lauterbrunnen Valley, or the other 4,000-foot assault up to Kleine Scheidegg (6,800 feet) for vistas up to the massive Jungfrau (13,642 feet). Either trip will reward you with a lodge at the summit and a wild downhill return.

St. Moritz, a famed ski area, is a real paradise for serious bikers. There are over 75 miles of tracks around the town, plus another 200 miles along the valley that were set up for winter Nordic skiing. Check out the Van D'Vina Trail, which is chiseled into a steep mountainside.

OUTFITTERS AND BIKE SHOPS

The Canadian adventure jocks behind Piste Artiste say they've ridden almost every summer day for the past five years, but have only

A LOUD, MILITANT NEUTRALITY

As you ride in the high mountains, you'll be amazed at the number of sonic booms you hear and the number of fighter jets that fill your eyeballs and rattle your components. In this famously neutral country, the military trains frequently and conspicuously. Why hasn't Switzerland entered war for centuries? Because its powerful army won't be goaded into others' problems. Service in the Swiss militia is compulsory for all males between the ages of 20 and 42. Switzerland does not maintain a standing army, however, so service consists of relatively short periods of training. Because rifles, uniforms, and other equipment are kept at home, Switzerland can mobilize completely within about 48 hours. If mobilized, the Swiss armed forces would include about 399,300 troops.

Because of the traditional neutrality of the country, Switzerland became the favored site for international conferences and the headquarters of many organizations. The main office of the International Red Cross was established there in 1863, as was that of the League of Nations following World War I (1914–1918). Switzerland was a league member but, after maintaining neutrality and harboring political refugees during World War II (1939–1945), the country refused to join the United Nations (UN) on the grounds that certain obligations of membership were incompatible with Swiss neutrality. It did, however, become a member of many agencies affiliated with the UN, and it maintains a permanent observer at UN headquarters. Switzerland's position of stalwart neutrality, however, as well as its pristine image, have been called into question by revelations about Swiss bankers' dealings with the Nazis during World War II.

scratched the surface of Champéry's immense terrain. Their tours take advantage of 23 chairlifts or let purists reward lung-busting climbs with stunning views and singletrack grin-fests.

Andiamo Adventours conducts whole-family adventures, and will customize its itineraries, but its specialty is mountainous excursions for "those comfortable with biking off-road." Its six-day Grindelwald trip takes in fine views of the three overwhelming north faces of Eiger, Moench, and Jungfrau—the Alps all-star team. The five-day Lake Lucerne tour guides you along moderate to challenging trails, including the Crazy Monk.

Cycleman is located in Gland, 15 minutes from Geneva and 20 minutes from Lausanne. It sells and services all the big bike industry names: Bianchi, Cannondale, K2, Merida, Time, Briko, Gore, and Northwave.

In Château d'Oex, head to Palaz Bike. Its knowledgeable staff will happily rent you the tools to attack the XC and DH courses from the '97 World Championships.

PISTE ARTISTE ©2000
  Box 146, 28 Old Brompton Rd.
  London SW7 3SS
  United Kingdom
  41-24-479-3489
  $100 per day

ANDIAMO ADVENTOURS
  Koehlerweid 6
  8260-Stein am Rhein
  Switzerland
  1-800-549-2363
  Fax: 831-477-2979
  41-052-741-5836
  $1,285 for 6 days

CYCLEMAN
  6 Avenue du Mont Blanc
  CH-1196 Gland, Switzerland
  41-022-364-55-00
  www.cycleman.ch

PALAZ BIKE
  41-26-924-42-51
  Palaz.bikayak@bluewin.ch

THE TRIALS OF HANS

Switzerland's most famous mountain biker traverses huge mountains, but became globally known for hopping small rocks. Hans "No Way" Rey is one of the pioneers of Trials and Extreme Mountain Biking. (Trials is mountain biking's black sheep cousin: the practice of performing controlled stunts on small, obstacle-ridden courses.) Rey shot to fame with his jump over a car on the 405 Freeway in Los Angeles, with his volcano dance in Hawaii, his underwater bungee jump, and his descent down the brutal steps of Machu Picchu. He's won dozens of titles, dominating Trials competition like Tiger Woods rules the PGA. At Atlanta in 1996, Rey was part of an Extreme Sports Act and performed in front of 3.5 billion viewers in the Olympic Closing Ceremonies.

Catching big air, Champéry. Don't underestimate the Alps' steep, rocky, sometimes downright severe downhills.

RECOMMENDED READING

■ *LONELY PLANET SWITZERLAND* (1997. $16.95. Lonely Planet.) The Bible of the young Alps traveler. The info is solid, and the authors have labored to find bargains in this most precious of nations.

■ *EUROPE BY BIKE*, Terry & Karen Whitehill (1992. $21.30. Peter Smith Pub.) Provides detailed itineraries for bike tourers, but Switzerland gets short shrift—it's only one of 11 countries profiled.

■ Guidebooks wouldn't work too well here anyway. The Alps are so craggy and convoluted that you will prefer a small-scale map. Mtb trail maps are easily found at most village tourist offices. But for good detail, get professional cartography. Mapmakers Kümmerly+Frey (0041-0-31-915-22 11; www.swissmaps.ch) are particularly recommended. The company's "Velokarten" is a bike-specific must-have.

■ *HEIDI*, Johanna Spyri (1998. $5.00. Gramercy.) The classic story of a young orphan sent to live with her grumpy grandfather in the Swiss Alps has charmed and intrigued readers since its original publication in 1880.

The Appalachian Mountains

Ride intense, technical singletrack—strings of dirt winding between tight spruce and maple trees, and over 15-inch-high roots and rocks.

S latyfork is like lots of small towns in eastern West Virginia: tucked into a narrow fold of the Appalachians, perched alongside a river that once supplied fish and sawmill power, and virtually hidden beneath a thick canopy of emerald woods. What separates Slatyfork from the Brandywines, Clover Licks, and other tiny burgs is the Elk River Touring Center—a lodge that has earned mention in publications from *Bon Appétit* to the East Coast's grittiest mountain bike 'zines.

Good vittles empower Elk River guests to tackle more than 200 miles of singletrack and fire roads in the surrounding woods. When my friends, Bob and Rich, and I visited not long ago, we were told that the best way to get a handle on West Virginia mountain biking was to ride the Gauley Mountain Trail with an Elk River guide. A challenging cult favorite of Eastern riders, Gauley Mountain is a string of dirt winding among tight

Slatyfork, West Virginia, where more than 200 miles of singletrack and fire roads await mountain bikers.

spruce and maple trees and over 15-inch-high roots and rocks.

Only a few miles long, Gauley defines the intense, technical single-track where progress can get derailed by circumstances small, large, and just plain weird. For instance, we veered too close to the singletrack's bushy walls, and got tagged by stinging nettles. When the scrapes began to itch and burn, our guide told us to rub them with jewelweed—a natural antidote to the nettles that grow nearby. Cool. Then Rich crushed his derailleur on a rock, which wasn't so cool, but we fixed it within 10 minutes. Moving on, we navigated a vast boulder garden to a twisting descent. The guide told us to "focus on the negative space between the rocks and around the logs. Try to flow down like water!" It worked, I guess. But given all the cells and skin we left behind, the "water" was the Ganges.

Still, it's an adrenaline kick to inch bike and self down an obstacle course masquerading as a trail. We were buzzing until we reached the next trail junction, where there stood a vandalized trail sign. Much malice had gone into its destruction. Evidently, some other trail users just don't want to share. Yet this teeth-marked, claw-scratched, utterly mutilated piece of wood seemed a bit extreme.

"The bear that did this really wanted to mark his territory," said our guide, while plucking tell-tale black hairs from the remaining shards of wood. "He probably peed on it, too."

Fortunately, the Appalachians of West Virginia are big enough—and wild enough—for biker and black bear alike. The "Mountain State" contains more than a million acres of national forest. About three-quarters of the state is forested. Much is thick, closely spaced, second-growth forest, but there are also airy groves of 300-year-old hemlocks. Both old and new recall the fairytale forests of Hansel and Gretel. Streams gurgle over rocky beds. Mosses and ferns line the forest floor. Above them loom rhododendron clusters so thick that old-timers claim to have lost horses in them.

As state boundaries go, few look more bizarre on a map than West Virginia's. What is that shape, anyway? An internal organ? Blame the vagaries of American history. When Virginia aligned with the Confederacy in the Civil War, 40 of its western counties split off and became a Union state. West Virginians sometimes bristle at the association with Virginia, but they have to admit that the initials are appropriate. Look at the letters "WV" and you're pretty much looking at

AT A GLANCE

TRIP LENGTH 6 days   PRICE RANGE (INDEPENDENT TRIP) $240

PHYSICAL CHALLENGE 1 2 3 ④ 5   PRICE RANGE (OUTFITTED GROUP TRIP) $800

MENTAL CHALLENGE 1 2 ③ 4 5   STAGING CITY Charleston, West Virginia

PRIME TIME April–early November   HEADS UP Full-suspension bikes needed for rocks and roots

the state's topography: punishing angles with seemingly no flats.

Here, long parallel mountain ridges, running from northeast to southwest, are separated by narrow valleys. The ridges are heavily forested and rise to between 3,000 and 4,000 feet. The steepest pitches are found along the state's eastern edge. While coal interests strip-mined other parts of the state, the Appalachian slopes drew loggers. It's said that West Virginia wood "built America's industrial revolution." The loggers hauled wood by train; their abandoned narrow-gauge railroads form many of the trails in the Monongahela National Forest.

Laced with more than 700 miles of marked recreation trails, the Monongahela offers mountain bike options up and down the eastern part of the state. In its Eden-like depths are the headwaters of major rivers like the Cheat and Gauley. The National Forest also contains the state's highest point, photogenic Seneca Rocks. Mountain bikers can enjoy incredible views of it from the revered North Fork Mountain Trail—a ridgetop single-track that skirts a small herd of bright white feral goats on its way to towering limestone ledges.

The Mountaineers we met were unabashedly proud to be living in West Virginia. Especially those who ride. The mountain bike scene/network/culture is as strong and vibrant as any better-known mecca. Thanks to the efforts of the West Virginia Mountain Bike Association, passion for the state's trails—and the desire to keep them open and unlogged—blazes hot and true.

West Virginia ranks only 34th in population among states, yet it boasts a 12-race state series and membership in the National Off-Road Biking Association (the governing body of mtb racing) is high. If the rest of the country joined at West Virginia's rate, NORBA would have 80,000 members instead of 30,000. Every year Elk River hosts the West Virginia Fat Tire festival, in which hundreds of riders camp in a five-acre field, play mountain bike polo, and patronize vendors like the French Rastafarian who cooks a mean banana crêpe.

Yep, banana crêpes in a place thought only to eat squirrel. West Virginia's always been the hilliest of hillbilly states—its rugged mountains seeming to keep prosperity at bay. During the 1950s the state's unemployment rate was the highest in the country, at three times the national average. More than 80,000 unemployed miners, with 170,000 dependents, lived a marginal existence. State relief laws had no adequate provisions to help them. As recently as 1985, the unemployment rate in the state was 15 percent.

Recreation dollars (from mountain biking, river rafting, rock climbing, and Civil War battle reenactments) have since washed over West Virginia. Yet this coal dust-stained state is kind of dark to begin with. There's depressing poverty. There are black bears. The state's shadowy forests saw the invention of what is now a global phenomenon: nighttime mtb racing. In West Virginia, you might as well give in to the dark.

We did. On our last night in West Virginia, we joined a night ride in the town of Fayetteville. The route, a collection of silky singletracks that

Opposite: The North Fork Mountain Trail, Monongahela National Forest. Above: Early-autumn valley fog, Pocahontas County.

must be sweet in daylight as well, wove down into the New River Gorge, passing various hardwoods and abandoned mine shafts that emit cool subterranean air.

Bob, Rich, and I agreed it was one of the best rides of our lives. Something to do with the sensations of exploring the dark on a dripping summer night, watching mist float through a 3,000-foot-deep river gorge, mud taking on the consistency of fudge, sodden leaves hissing in your wake, nostril hairs standing on end, feeling like you'd just snarfed down a virility stew of bat wing, tiger nut, and rhino horn while rain patters against the forest canopy and your friends holler with mirth.

As the West Virginia state flag puts it, *Montani semper liberi*. Mountaineers are always free.

WHAT TO EXPECT

West Virginia is located entirely within the Appalachian Mountain range. More than 75 percent of the state is forested, and there are nearly 2,000 miles of streams and rivers. Yet the natural wonders are hardly remote: 45 percent of the United States population lives within a 500-mile radius of the capital city of Charleston. Wags pronounce West Virginia the southernmost Northern state, the northernmost Southern state, the easternmost Western state, and the westernmost Eastern state.

Maybe the Appalachians, which have been around as long as any mountains on earth, have grown a bit testy in their old age. They frequently impede mtb progress with roots and rocks—big ones that can turn riding into a series of semi-controlled ricochets. Riders accustomed to the West's fast, smooth trails will need to recalibrate their notions of distance and time: In West Virginia, an eight-mile ride can take three hours.

In short, the trails are bumpy. Yes, skilled riders can navigate them on a hardtail. But full-suspension bikes were invented for terrain like this. Bring your own, or rent one, and you'll truly enjoy the tight, technical singletrack that defines Eastern mountain biking.

The western slope of the Appalachians catches a lot of storms, so prepare for rain. Bring a jacket even in summer. When Washington, D.C. and Pittsburgh are steaming, the 4,000-foot ridges of West Virginia are often refreshingly cool—and sometimes cold. The good news is that summer annoyances such as ticks and poison ivy don't exist. Consider riding West Virginia in the fall: With hardwoods such as oak, yellow poplar, maple, birch, beech, black walnut, hickory, and gum lacing the hillsides, the foliage is spectacular.

Most of the prime rides are in the Monongahela National Forest (304-779-4334), which occupies 900,000 acres on the eastern side of the state. The West Virginia Division of Tourism (800-CALL-WVA or www.state.wv.us/tourism) is extremely bike-friendly, and can provide you with maps and lists of outfitters. Pocahontas

BUNKER MENTALITY

The Monongahela's cool summers made eastern West Virginia a fashionable resort for rich planters of the Old South. Then and now, the five-star Greenbrier Hotel attracts visitors from all parts of the world. It looks and feels like a genteel bastion of luxury. But the Cold War profoundly changed the Greenbrier. During the 1950s, bunkers were constructed beneath the hotel for members of the United States Congress to use in case Russia unleashed its nuclear arsenal. The existence of the shelter was once one of the nation's best-kept secrets.

Stream Crossing, Snowshoe Mountain Resort, Pocahontas County.

County also likes mountain bikers; call 800-336-7009 to get the skinny on its services. For general West Virginia biking information, surf to www.bicyclewv.com.

LODGING

The Elk River Touring Center makes a fine first stop. The trail network is extensive, the maps are excellent, the rooms are clean, and the food is tasty. The main lodge contains 10 rooms, with either private or shared baths. For families or larger groups, there are also three cabins: They sleep six and come with kitchens, living rooms, stereos, TVs, and VCRs. ERTC's renowned Fat Tire Festival happens in late July. Contact 304-572-3771, www.ertc.com, or elk@neumedia.net for all things Elk.

In Fayetteville, stay at the White Horse Bed & Breakfast (304-574-1400), a spectacular mansion owned by nice people who know how to cook.

THE RIDES

Plantation Trail, the Canaan Valley's most famous, is located just outside of Davis. It's a yin-yang of a trail. The dark, foreboding forest it navigates is counterbalanced by the beauty of the white-flowered rhododendrons and other natural wonders. Even if you don't enjoy the woods' Brothers Grimm ambiance, you'll probably like the wild blueberries, the bear paw prints that go along with them, or the steep descents that require a chess-like ability to think ahead and link large root drops.

Props Run was named one of the finest downhills in the United States by *Mountain Bike* magazine. From Slatyfork's Gauley Mountain Road, it slips between two young spruces and into a forest so thick you could wear night-vision goggles at noon. Then comes 1,900 vertical feet of descent, down steep and rocky terrain, that evokes the classic paradox of hypertechnical rides: feeling like you're about to kill yourself, and enjoying it immensely.

The Cranberry Back Country, on the other hand, is 26,000 acres of grassy meadows linked by buff, serpentine singletrack. You can zip over pine-needle carpets without interruption from rattling components or other trail users. In Cranberry, 25 miles southwest of Slatyfork, the tree canopy is so high and narrow, you feel like you're riding into a cathedral. The light comes in like through stained-glass windows.

Snowshoe Mountain Resort (304-572-5252; www.snowshoemtn.com), a ski resort in winter, opens its 11,000 acres to mountain bikers after the snow melts. A full-service operation, Snowshoe offers 75 miles of trails, shops, guided tours, equipment rentals, and shuttle service to the mountain's summit. Snowshoe is also home to The 24 Hours of Snowshoe race, the original all-day/all-night relay. Its unique format has been imitated all over North America. To learn more about the race, usually held in June, call 304-259-5533.

OUTFITTERS AND BIKE SHOPS

The Elk River Touring Center boasts its own shop, and it runs a variety of group and individual tours, from beginners' rides to four-day singletrack epics.

In the Canaan Valley/Davis area, head to Blackwater Bikes. Ridge Rider isn't merely the best shop in Fayetteville, it's also a great deli, coffee shop, and shuttle operator. Ridge Rider also rents high-tech Niterider lighting systems, meaning you can paddle the New River during the day, then ride the trails in its gorge at night.

ELK RIVER TOURING CENTER

HC 69 Box 7
Slatyfork WV 26291
304-572-3771
www.ertc.com
$400 for 4 days

WHEN IT'S IMPOLITE TO STARE

Not only did West Virginia foster the all-night race (the oft-imitated 24 Hours of Snowshoe), it also gave birth to one of competitive cycling's most disgusting traditions. We're talking, of course, about the infamous Team Hugh Jass.

Most of the five-person teams at a 24-hour race behave predictably: They take turns riding laps of the 10-plus-mile course, then exchange batons, relay-style, with the next rider waiting in the start tent. Team Hugh Jass, though, doesn't just exchange batons. They exchange tight lycra bike shorts. The same pair every time.

So five different guys ride hundreds of miles over the course of 24 hours in a single pair of shorts. There are frequent wedgies. "Grody" doesn't begin to describe it.

RIDGE RIDER

102 Keller Avenue
Fayetteville, WV 25840
800-890-BIKE, 304-574-BIKE
www.wvbike.com
$95 per day

RECOMMENDED READING

■ *OFF THE BEATEN TRACK VOLUME VI: A GUIDE TO MOUNTAIN BIKING IN WEST VIRGINIA,* Jim Parham (1995. $12.95. WMC Publishing.) This reads a lot cleaner than its title does. Sold in most W.V. bike shops.

■ The Adventure Cycling Association (406-721-1776, email: acabike@aol.com) distributes a detailed map of rides in the Monongahela.

■ *HILL DAUGHTER: NEW & SELECTED POEMS,* Louise McNeill (1991. $29.95. University of Pittsburgh Press.) Louise McNeill was born in 1911 in Pocahontas County, West Virginia, on a farm that her family had lived on for nine generations. She was appointed Poet Laureate of West Virginia in 1979. She died in 1993.

Top: Headwaters Trail, Russell Holt farm near Snowshoe Ski area, Gauley Mountain. Above: Overlooking Germany Valley, not far from Seneca Rock.

The Andes

A ride that begins on a scree slope at 18,000 feet can end in machete jungle bashing; velvety smooth llama pastures tumble into Inca staircases.

As my friend Aaron Teasdale tells it, "Alistair and I had taken the old jeep as far up as the Andes would allow, to around 14,000 feet, but the pass we sought was still a good hike higher. As we stepped out of the battered Land Cruiser, two young boys jumped down from the rear bumper and offered to porter our gear. They'd leapt on a few miles back as the jeep passed their village; the famed Takesi Trail starts here and they were used to trekkers passing through en route. Except we weren't trekkers. We had come to ride.

"An hour of bike-on-back hiking—well ok, so I paid the little urchins $2 to carry mine—and we crested a rocky, sun-blasted saddle. The nether opened to a great valley framed by sharp ridges that spilled off frozen peaks and sank into the labyrinthine blue depths of misty cloud forest ravines and, in the distance, the soft white cloud cover of the Amazon. Tumbling through it all was

Heading into the high country and the famed Takesi Trail, with its 9,000-plus foot descent.

an ancient trail—and nearly 10,000 feet below, at ride's end, a rickety wooden bridge spanning a rush of whitewater awaited our arrival."

This is Bolivia, the undiscovered mountain bike paradise of the Americas. La Paz-based New Zealander Alistair Matthew had been Aaron's guide for several weeks of passes and peaks, first descents and some of the biggest, wildest downhills on earth. His favorite was the granddaddy kingpin of Bolivian downhills—the Takesi Trail. One of a mind-boggling network of Inca, or pre-Inca, trails that web Bolivia's mountains, it cuts up and across a 15,200-foot pass before plunging through cleavered cloud forest valleys for more than 9,000 ferociously technical feet in less than 17 miles. No, that's not a typo. A 9,000-plus foot descent down an Inca trail. On a bike. Bring your camera.

The highest and most isolated country in South America, Bolivia was called "The Himalaya of the New World" by European explorers. It has approximately 1,000 peaks higher than 16,000 feet. Many of these plummet almost directly into the Amazon Basin via lush, jaw-droppingly steep canyons and valleys. One of the poorest and least developed nations in the world, Bolivia has foot and llama paths older than history lacing through it. Some regions have yet to be accurately mapped, much less mountain biked. For die-hard adventure riders, this is the promised land.

The first thing you notice upon arriving at the La Paz, Bolivia, airport is the wall of spectacular ice-capped peaks in the distance. The second thing you notice is the distinct lack of oxygen in the air. Perched at 13,000 feet, the La Paz International Airport is, by far, the world's highest and La Paz itself, a thousand feet below, is the highest world capital. Set in a sprawling badland canyon against a backdrop of glaciated alps, it's also one of the planet's most spectacular cities. The great Andean spine dominating views to the north and east is the Cordillera Real. Riddled with Inca trails and 20,000-foot summits, it's the most readily accessible chunk of Andes from La Paz—several 10,000-foot descents start only a short drive from the city. A day in a jeep can bring you to any number of other far-flung, *Raiders of the Lost Ark*-style riding stashes.

Long known more for its turbulent past— 188 coups in 157 years; yup, that's a record—and robust cocaine output, Bolivia has settled into a

---

AT A GLANCE

TRIP LENGTH 14 days

PHYSICAL CHALLENGE 1 2 3 4 (5)

MENTAL CHALLENGE 1 2 3 4 (5)

PRIME TIME May–September

PRICE RANGE (INDEPENDENT TRIP) $300

PRICE RANGE (OUTFITTED GROUP TRIP) $900

STAGING CITY La Paz, Bolivia

HEADS UP Bandits are less common than elsewhere in South America, but it still makes sense to keep your money and affluence hidden relatively stable democracy as of late. While La Paz sports skyscrapers, vegetarian restaurants, and the occasional Mercedes, the rest of Bolivia operates on a much lower frequency. It is now considered one of the safest countries in Latin America for travelers. The Bolivian people are, on the whole, sweet, quick to smile, and supremely laid back. This is good, unless you happen to be in a hurry. Bolivians are never in a hurry. In fact they seem to live their lives completely independent of bothersome notions like time. Which is great if you are a hard-driving yuppie stockbroker burnout looking for a new way of life, but frustrating as hell if you are trying to get anything done. The only solution is not to be in a hurry.

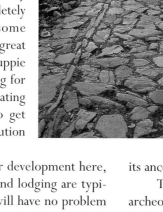

There's little money or development here, which means travel, food, and lodging are typically very cheap. Dirtbags will have no problem getting by on $10–$20 a day. Quality standards vary, and travelers to Bolivia should brace themselves for this. Bolivia is not Colorado. Accommodations are simple. People speak Spanish, if you're lucky. In the countryside they often speak Aymara and Quechua, ancient languages of Inca and pre-Inca civilizations. Indeed, the culture here may be the most intact, that is, the least Westernized, of any South American nation. This alone is good reason to visit.

Hell, the Takesi Trail alone is good reason to visit. Says Aaron, "From the pass Alistair and I shot down mile after mile of off-the-back-of-the-seat steep, zigzag-ging, stone paths and steps. The valley walls grew higher and higher, until we came to the village of Takesi. Llamas grazed and a family tending a patch of potatoes tried not to stare as we passed." Little more than a small cluster of stone and thatch huts, life there has changed little since its ancestors built this trail.

The Incas ruled here 500 years ago, but archeologists agree that many of the trails in Bolivia predate their empire. Little is known about these early civilizations, but it's clear the Incas learned much from them; the stone paving in Bolivia bears much similarity to the great Inca

Above: Ancient Inca pavement on the Takesi Trail. Opposite: The Corioco road features 10-foot widths and 1000-foot drops.

BOLIVIAN MARCHING POWDER

To much of the world Bolivia is synonymous with cocaine. And with good reason—it's the unspoken foundation of the nation's economy. By far Bolivia's most lucrative export, it's been estimated that a full one-third of the country's workforce is dependent on cocaine-related commerce. This should be no surprise in this, one of the poorest countries in the world—

cocaine's an easy cash cow. As long as there's demand, farmers here will gladly supply.

The coca plant, cocaine's source, is considered sacred to most Bolivians, and many, particularly in the country, chew wads of coca leaves daily. Coca tea is mild, pleasant, and widely available. It can also soothe the effects of altitude.

trails of Peru in both construction and grandeur. But in Bolivia, wild ungoverned Bolivia, you can ride them.

When Aaron plunged down the Takesi's twisted path, his guide suffered a total front-disk-brake meltdown. "Well this is going to be interesting," Alistair said, and had to ride the lower half with only a rear brake. The air turned liquid, trailside grew into cloud forest, and the paved path transformed into a thin dirt seam overhanging the jungled depths below. Says Aaron, "And we rode and rode, picking and jabbing forever downward until muscles I didn't know I had screamed for mercy and blisters broke out on my braking fingers.

"After crossing the river at trail's end and riding the last stretch of dirt road to our jeep—twilight air turning a cool misty blue, jungle spilling and arching over our heads—fireflies sparked along the greenery like dancing beacons. Above, back from where we'd come, a snow-mantled peak emerged through dark blue clouds and night's eager stars began pricking the sky. Though we were utterly and completely shattered, all thoughts of 'must...reach...jeep' were lost in the pure perfection of the moment.

"Waking up the next morning in a two-dollar room in the village of Yanacachi, a breeze blowing the songs of birds and frogs through the open window above my bed, I looked out across towering green valley walls and smiled as my mind flashed back on the previous day. Damn if I hadn't just ridden the best downhill on the planet. And I had the blisters on my fingers to prove it."

WHAT TO EXPECT

Bolivia sits dead center on the South American continent, landlocked and bordered by Peru, Chile, Argentina, Paraguay, and Brazil. American Airlines offers the best air service to La Paz, with daily flights from Miami. There are no national tourist organizations to speak of.

This is frontier-style, high-adventure riding at its finest. Be self-sufficient. You will not be rescued. Be fit. These rides demand it. A good strategy is to spend a week chilling in La Paz upon arrival, as your body needs time to adjust to the (lack of) oxygen. Altitude is a serious factor in riding here. Work your way up to the higher rides slowly. Once you've gotten your lungs, do some warm-up rides from La Paz. There's plenty of technical slum riding, or check out the singletrack to Muela Del Diablo (the Devil's Molar) just outside of town.

Consider packing lightweight body armor. Rides here are often obscenely technical and witch doctors are the norm in the more remote areas. The best strategy is to avoid serious injury.

Be prepared for surprise intestinal guests. Wild stints of volcanic expulsions are the norm in Bolivia, where hygiene is a trend that hasn't quite caught on and the bacteria live free. Every traveler here gets sick at least once, but it typically lasts only a day or two.

It can be hard to find basic items in Bolivia. If, for instance, you lose your fleece, destroy your headset, and snap your Oakleys, all in the first three days of arriving, you are up a certain well-known creek. If, on the other hand, you need llama fetuses, coca leaves, or Panoasonic (sic) radios, simply head to the chaotic street markets. In other words: bring all your own gear, for bike and body.

Outside of coca, mining has traditionally been Bolivia's economic backbone. While much of Bolivia's mineral wealth has now been tapped, mining's legacy to mountain bikers remains in the form of a vast network of remote mining roads. They can provide a welcome respite from the oft brutal trails, and can be excellent rides in their own right. They also open the door to the possibility of serious back-

On a footpath along the Corioco road, called "The World's Most Dangerous Road" by the Inter-American Bank.

country, high-mountain touring.

The rainy season lasts from November to March, give or take a few weeks, when daily downpours are the norm. The cool sunny days that are prevalent the rest of the year are ideal for riding. It gets cold and windy in the high mountains and muggy in the cloud and rain forest year round.

LODGING

In La Paz cheap, clean, hostel-style lodging can be found at El Careterro (591-2-322-233). Also recommended are the Happy Days Hostel and Hostel Naira, which are comfortable and centrally located. For truly posh digs head to El Ray Palace (591-2-393-016), where both your mind and your wallet will forget you're in the Third World.

THE RIDES

As for the trails, like Bolivia itself they are rugged and incredibly varied. A ride may begin on a scree slope at 18,000 feet and end in machete-required jungle bashing; velvety smooth llama pastures may tumble into rocky Inca staircases. Shouldering your bike and hiking is an ever-present possibility. As these ancient byways are still primary routes for many rural Bolivians, nearly every village, canyon, and many high mountain passes are interconnected. User conflicts are not an issue—just let the damn alpacas by. And watch out for llama dung. When fresh and stepped in it has incredible cement-like properties and will take a very, very long time to clean out of your SPDs.

A good welcome-to-Bolivia ride is the La Paz-to-Corioco road. Don't let the "road" part fool you. It's a ragged, serpentine chute of mud and dust that rockets down 11,000 feet in 49 miles, from a frozen, desolate pass through cloud and cloud forest and waterfalls that land mid-road, into muggy tangles of jungle that spill over the roadside like groping green tentacles. Call it road biking, Bolivian style. Tagged the "World's Most Dangerous Road" by the Inter-American Bank, it features 10-foot widths, sheer 1,000-foot drops, and a multitude of small white crosses to remind drivers of the motorcycles, jeeps, and buses full of people that routinely pitch off its precipices. In short, it's a bitch to drive, but a rip-roaring hoot of a ride.

The downright pitiful ski area on 17,695-foot Mount Chacaltaya (just outside La Paz) is technically the highest in the world. If it's worth skiing, it's only for that reason. A better bet is to hike from the "lodge" to the summit with your bike and shoot the massive scree slope on the eastern flank of the mountain. There's an old mining road below that is a virtual BMX course of banked turns and perfectly sloped airs that contours snow-fringed lakes and towering cliff faces on its way back to La Paz. The many trails down the canyon walls into the city can be steep and thrilling.

The quiet, idyllic village of Sorata, a half-day's drive from La Paz, is nestled in palm trees at the base of an ice-covered 21,000-foot massif. It's the kind of place a writer could spend his later days taking walks and filling note-

Above: Shooting the scree slope on the eastern flank of 17,695-foot Mount Chacaltaya.
Opposite: The Takesi Trail, the ride you'd do if you knew you were going to die tomorrow.

The Takesi Trail: mile after mile of zigzagging Inca-engineered stone paths and steps.

books. It's also the kind of place a mountain biker could go absolutely nuts bombing single-track down the surrounding mountainsides. There are many riding options here and the setting is as fine as any in Bolivia.

The trail from Lago Tuni to the Zongo Valley is one of Bolivia's best. A challenging hike over a 16,500-foot pass is rewarded with dramatic views of the surrounding peaks and a never-ending singletrack descent through a gaping maw of a valley beset by icy, plaque-encrusted, black granite canines. It ends many hours later deep in cloud forest.

The Takesi Trail is the ride you'd do if you knew you were going to die tomorrow and you could choose any trail on earth. Take the steepest, rockiest trail you've ever ridden, combine it with the tightest, most exposed trail you've ever ridden. Throw in the ghosts of an ancient civilization and the biggest, most savagely beautiful landscape imaginable. Shake, stir, and descend for 10 straight hours. That's the Takesi.

OUTFITTERS AND BIKE SHOPS

Gravity Assisted Mountain Biking, Alistair Matthew's guiding outfit, is the only choice for the hardcore biker. No one knows Bolivia's network of foot trails and Incan and pre-Incan pathways better. Probably because no one else is riding them. He has a fully supported, 13-day trip that covers the rides mentioned above and a variety of ripping single-day trips down the World's Most Dangerous Road, Chacaltaya, etc. Customized expeditions, including mellower jeep-road tours, are also an option.

Colorado-based KE Adventure Travel runs a 19-day, fully-supported tour every summer. Largely focused on jeep and mining roads, it covers an incredible variety of terrain from the high mountains to the deep jungle.

La Paz has a Trek shop, Bicicar, that carries sundry parts and has somewhat knowledgeable mechanics. Alistair's crew can also order parts and perform overhauls, etc.

GRAVITY ASSISTED MOUNTAIN BIKING
c/o America Tours S.R.L.
Av. 16 de Julio #1490
Edificio Avenida
Ground Floor, Office #9
La Paz, Bolivia
591-2-374-204
www.gamb.acslp.org
Custom prices

KE ADVENTURE TRAVEL—USA
1131 Grand Avenue
Glenwood Springs, CO 81601
Toll Free: 800-497-9675
970-384-0001
ww.keadventure.com
$2,725 for 19 days

BICICAR
591-2-77-22-17

RECOMMENDED READING

■ *BOLIVIA HANDBOOK,* Alan Murphy (1997. $21.95. Footprint Handbooks.) Updated biannually. The best and most up to date all-around guidebook to Bolivia.

■ *TREKKING IN BOLIVIA,* Yossi Brain (1997. $16.95. The Mountaineers.) The authoritative guide to the trails and remote regions of Bolivia. The best option in lieu of an actual mtb guide.

■ The South American Explorers is an invaluable resource for travelers and explorers, offering maps, books, and trip reports (607-277-0488, explorer@samexplo.org, www.samexplo.org).

■ *THE LOST WORLD,* Sir Arthur Conan Doyle (1977. $4.00. Buccaneer Books.) Originally published in 1912, this science fiction classic describes a prehistoric world hidden deep in mountainous rain forest. Based on the explorer Colonel Percy Harrison Fawcett's early descriptions of a remote corner of the Bolivian jungle.

Kathmandu Valley & Pokhara

*Tracks, trails, and back roads lead to medieval towns,
17,000-foot vistas, and the Indiana Jones fantasies fostered
by crossing yawning chasms on rickety footbridges.*

In the 1960s, not long after Edmund Hillary and Tenzing Sherpa first climbed Mount Everest, the airy kingdom of Nepal became famous for its trekking. Inspired by the photos and accounts of pioneering mountaineers, trekkers began hiking to the bases of the highest peaks in the world. Trekkers don't make technical climbs: They hardly need to, since they can drink in the intense beauty of the Himalaya just by following trails that have been used for communication and trade for centuries.

While trekking, visitors to Nepal experience pretty villages, churning rivers, bucolic forests, and sacred mountains. Hundreds of thousands of people trek in Nepal every year. It's little wonder, then, that mountain bikers looking to explore Nepal in the 1980s decided to follow the same sublime trails trod by trekkers.

They promptly found that mountain bikes and trekking trails mix just as pleasantly as do

Harvested rice fields, Bugamati Village, near Kathmandu, Nepal.

human skin and water buffalo horns. Because Nepali trekking trails contain frequent stretches of sharp stone staircases with big, sharp, stone steps, riders who attempted them wound up carrying their bikes 90 percent of the time!

Mountain bikers in Nepal now laugh at those early misadventures. They've discovered that Nepal boasts a vast network of rideable paths. Tracks, trails, and back roads lead to medieval towns, 17,000-foot vistas, and the Indiana Jones fantasies fostered by crossing yawning chasms on rickety footbridges. Mountain bikers can follow narrow yak trails or the ancient routes of Trans-Himalayan traders. They can undertake multi-day tours around areas rarely visited by tourists. In short, the trekkers can keep their rocky chunks of nastiness for themselves. Cyclists prefer to go where the porters and incontinent goats will not.

Some in Kathmandu's adventure guide community pronounce Nepal an upcoming mountain bike mecca. It certainly mixes all the classic ingredients: staggering mountain scenery, rolling foothills, countless miles of serene dirt, and an ancient, exotic culture.

First settled in the seventh century, Nepal remained a little-known, little-visited mountain kingdom for eons. Westerners had shadowy impressions—but little knowledge— of this remote inland sanctuary where people decorated walls with erotic carvings and prayed to monkey gods. As recently as 1947, Nepal was the largest inhabited country on earth yet to be explored by Europeans. The life expectancy of the average citizen was a prehistoric 24 years.

Opening its borders didn't make Nepal much simpler to understand. In terms of religion, Nepal is officially Hindu, but it blends in Buddhist and tantric influences as well. As such, it worships 30 million gods and encourages Sadhus—long-haired seekers who throw away jobs and normalcy in order to walk Nepal on lifelong spiritual searches. At once a time machine and a magic carpet, Nepal sweeps you along crooked, timeworn streets flanked by irregular, multi-roofed pagodas, stupas, and stone sculptures, and into rooms cluttered with horror-eyed masks, spinning prayer wheels, and trippy *thangka* scrolls. Muttered chants, esoteric tantric hymns and Nepalese music, whether it be the twang of a four-stringed *saringhi* or the plaintive notes of a flute, hang in the air. The very mystique of Nepal attracted masses of hippies (the so-called "Grand Tour") in the 1960s and '70s. Alas, no amount of local hashish can make sense of the inscrutable. Take, for example, the ubiquitous Nepali teahouse poster

---

AT A GLANCE

TRIP LENGTH	11 days	
PHYSICAL CHALLENGE	1 2 3 ④ 5	
MENTAL CHALLENGE	1 2 3 4 ⑤	
PRIME TIME	December–April	
PRICE RANGE (INDEPENDENT TRIP)	$250	
PRICE RANGE (OUTFITTED GROUP TRIP)	$1,100	
STAGING CITY	Kathmandu, Nepal	
HEADS UP	Nonviolent theft is common	

Nepal: Tracks, trails, back roads and 17,000-foot vistas. This span was pummeled by boulders loosened by torrential rain.

with these English words: "Home is the place where if you have to go there, they have to take you in." Westerners may never comprehend certain customs—for instance, the fact that Nepalis don't like to give negative answers. Thus, they'll give you wrong directions if they fear the right ones might disappoint you.

Nepal has always represented a dividing line between civilizations and cultures. Here the plains of the subcontinent climb up to the high plateau of Tibet, the languages and people of India give way to those of China. Asia is a place that you want to throw adjectives at—exotic, surreal, putrid, mystical, steamy, enormous. But in truth, you can describe it using just nouns, verbs, and assorted articles and prepositions: Beggar swings carcass of dog at passersby. Eight-year-old girls carry iron cooking pots by tying hemp tumplines around their heads. Donkeys wearing bells, baubles, and woven headdresses lead 20-beast pack trains up 18-inch-wide trail.

The capital of Kathmandu, a fascinating mess of a city, cloaks untold oddities in the shadows of 500-year-old temples. Three-wheeled auto-rickshaws with Buddha's eyes (all three of them) painted on the bumper. Cremation pyres. Drying goat blood, from an earlier sacrifice for the god of the day. Liquids that may or may not be sewage. To bike in the congestion of Kathmandu takes guts and a strong tolerance for exhaust. But head outside the city, toward the 8,000-foot walls of the bowl-like Kathmandu valley, and you'll find rides not soon forgotten.

A short spin lands you in a world of wooded slopes, sleepy villages, and hidden temples. Keep ascending toward the valley rim and you'll meet ridgetop singletracks that reveal what's, literally, the most spectacular backdrop in the world: the Nepalese Himalaya, starring 8 of Earth's 10 tallest peaks. Many rides include heart-stopping downhills with dozens of hairpin turns and singletracks that thread through emerald-green rice fields.

Riders can explore a variety of single-day rides in both Kathmandu and Pokhara, a charming lakeside city that serves as a jumping-off point for many famous treks. However, mtb adventurers are most impressed with Nepal's long, multi-day tours. Consider the 600-mile epic from Kathmandu to Lhasa, Tibet. It takes two to three weeks, traverses the backbone of the Himalaya, crosses six major passes, offers views of Mount Everest's seldom-climbed North Face, and connects two of Asia's most engaging cities.

Between the historic monasteries, flowing spans of prayer flags, and simple oxygen deprivation, Kathmandu-to-Lhasa feels less like a bike ride and more like a vision quest.

Some of the Grand Tour's leftover hippies complain that Nepal has changed too drastically in the last quarter century (since the Grand Tour, the country did become a democracy and swell its population by hundreds of thousands). Even younger globetrotters fret that Nepal has "been done," that the immense popularity of adventure travel and the immense sales of *Into Thin Air* have robbed Nepal of its mystique. Okay, but the Himalayas haven't gotten any smaller. They still repel civilization. They still insist that stoves be fueled by yak dung. They still laugh at the mere mention of asphalt.

Rest assured, Nepal will rejigger your notions of travel. The kingdom doesn't accommodate rigid, Western-centric brains. Indeed, it runs stampedes of sacred cows across such brains until they're once again soft, pliable, and capable of wonder. Mountain bikes accelerate the process. When you ride a sturdy, knobby-tired machine, you go anywhere at any time. More important, you escape backpacker enclaves, clogged trekking trails, and other manifestations of the tourists' Nepal

Veer off Nepal's beaten paths. Even if the country as a whole remains ultimately unfathomable, the adventurous rider will unearth small meanings and keen insights. This is what exploring the subcontinent is all about. Here in the land of yoga and meditation, sweat and heavy breathing often accompany the process of discovery.

Above: Pokhara, Nepal, with Macchapuchhare in background. Overleaf: Buddhist monks take turns riding at a monastery founded by the fifth Dalai Lama and located at an elevation of 10,000 feet.

Primate view of the rooftops of Kathmandu.

WHAT TO EXPECT

The nation of Nepal sits between India and China in south Asia. All international flights land and clear customs in Kathmandu. Don't bother renting a car in Nepal—the cabs are plentiful and cheap. Not to mention that Nepalis drive on the left and that traffic can be maddening.

If performance matters to you, bring your own bike. Should a customs officials ask for import duty, explain that you are a tourist and the bike will leave the country with you. They may give you a receipt to include in your passport to make sure you do not sell your bike in the country.

According to *Encarta Encyclopedia,* "Nepal has a relatively underdeveloped network of roads . . . the main means of transportation is the network of footpaths and trails that interlace the mountains and valleys." Indeed, bike touring outfits keep turning up long stretches of previously hidden singletracks. Since trekking is a major industry here, Nepal moved easily into the mountain bike tourism game. Veteran adventure guides quickly added riding to their menus. These days, anyone with a computer and a search engine can sign up for dozens of Nepali rides.

The best riding takes place around the cities of Kathmandu and Pokhara (located 75 miles northwest of the capital). Both access idyllic villages, with lots of trails and Himalaya views. There are also jungle roads in the Terai lowlands; mountain biking is an excellent way to reach Royal Chitwan National Park and its tigers and elephants. If you want to explore via bike, the northwest part of Nepal remains raw and challenging.

Trekking in Mustang. It didn't take long for bikers to learn that trekking trails don't suit cycling.

Many trails are narrow walkways and are not shown on maps, so you need a good sense of direction when venturing out without a guide. Make sure you know the name of the next village on your route so locals can point you in the right direction.

Perhaps the best time to visit Nepal is October and November, the start of the dry season that runs until May. The temperatures are pleasant, and the recent rains have cleared the air

WHERE'S THE BEEF?

Because Hindus consider them sacred, cows get off scot-free in Nepal. Still, you can sit in a Kathmandu restaurant and order a steak. Why? Because water buffalo aren't considered sacred at all. When biking Nepal, you see lots of water buffalo bulking up for the slaughter. They stand in puddles of their own waste, chewing their cud while a dirty white, viscous foam flecks their snouts. What strikes you most about the water buffalo is the crazy way their horns bend. Some horns curl into valentines, some point up like tiaras, and others fade down their necks like dreadlocks. There's simply no consistency, and I think this is why Hindus withhold the much-coveted "sacred" designation.

Mountain biking in the Himalaya is not only about mountains; vast, lonely valleys separate ranges, providing the chance to acclimate.

and made the hills verdant. The wet, or monsoon, season runs from June to September. Keep in mind that Kathmandu is on approximately the same latitude as Miami. It's often quite warm, and it never sees snow. But mountain bikers can climb from the lowland jungle to higher than 17,000 feet in Nepal. Needlesss to say, there are huge temperature variations. If you plan to ride the high country, bring cold weather gear.

Contact the Nepal Tourism Board (www.welcomenepal.com) or the Nepali Diplomatic Office (415-434-1111) for information.

LODGING

The Borderland Adventure Centre (977-1-425836; info@borderlands.net; www.borderlands.net) is a mountain bike retreat located just 10 miles south of the Tibetan border and a mere three hours from Kathmandu. Borderland says its lodge and attractions have "a mystical force so great that it immediately transports its guests to another place and time when life was far less complicated."

Nirvana Garden-Hotel (977-1-256200; nirvana@wlink.com.np) is located in a tranquil oasis right in the heart of Thamel, Kathmandu's bustling tourist area. It boasts nice balconies for overlooking the capital, plus a lush garden replete with a rocky waterfall and a profusion of flowers, trees, and birds.

THE RIDES

The Balaju-Kakani ride is one of the Kathmandu Valley's finest. From the bifurcation at Balaju (a Kathmandu suburb), start climbing northwest. The entire 14-mile trip to the hill resort of Kakani offers a magnificent view of the valley. The route passes through forests, waterfalls, and meadows. There are several restaurants on the way if you feel like resting or munching on some snacks.

Pokhara to Kathmandu: Linking together a maze of singletrack village paths between the two cities, this is a brilliant multi-day trip. Head eastward, via the Marsyangdi and Trisuli valleys and the ridge-top town of Gorkha, on trails that have seen few mountain bikes. The finale comes after a mile-high climb up to the rim of the Kathmandu Valley, with breathtaking views of most of the Nepal Himalaya. From there, it's all downhill to the capital. (KE Adventures leads a well-designed Pokhara to Kathmandu tour.)

Pokhara to Sarangkot is a challenging day trip. Ride lakeside toward the mountains, staying north at intersections. The ride becomes a singletrack that hugs the edge of the Phewa Tal lake. Pass the first turn to Sarangkot and ride singletrack into the Harpan Khola river valley. Riding through Kaski, you'll gain a ridge with spectacular views of Himalayan classics, including the sacred, never-summited peak of Machhapuchhare, which is shaped like a massive fish tail.

OUTFITTERS AND BIKE SHOPS

Keep in mind, there are no "real" biking shops or outfitters in Nepal; only agencies for trips. These places may be able to help you with parts and tune-ups, but supplies will be limited. For longer trips, bring the gear you would use at home. If disaster does strike, take heart that Nepali mechanics improvise well.

Colorado-based KE Adventure Travel is a well-respected Himalayan outfitter. Its highlights include a singletrack-heavy route from Pokhara to Kathmandu.

Bikeman leads a variety of tours in the Kathmandu area, including a great 5-day exploration of the valley rim.

KE ADVENTURE TRAVEL–USA

1131 Grand Avenue
Glenwood Springs, CO 81601
800-497-9675
970-384-0001
www.keadventure.com
$1,800 for 13 days

BIKEMAN NEPAL

P.O. Box 3380
Jyatha-Thamel
Kathmandu, Nepal
977-1-240633
http://web.singnet.com.sg/~bikeman/Contact_Us/a_Rectangle_2.gif
$400 for 4 days

RECOMMENDED READING

■ *LONELY PLANET NEPAL* (2000. $24.95. Lonely Planet.) Makes a fine general guidebook.
■ *THE SNOW LEOPARD,* Peter Matthiessen (1996. $13.95. Penguin.) Details the author's two-headed quest in Nepal: to search for the elusive Himalayan snow leopard (the rarest of the great cats) and to find answers for his deteriorating personal life back home. Set in the northwest part of Nepal, *The Snow Leopard* lyrically describes the perils of climbing treacherously high mountains, the calming serenity of Buddhism, the infectious joy of Sherpas, and the soul-crushing sight of crippled children.

The North

In the abrupt tropical mountains between teeming Bangkok and the mysterious Golden Triangle resides a culture so exotic it's been called the "Fourth World."

"Welcome you to Thailand, the land of smile. There are many interesting things in Thailand. Culture, Traditional, Art, Temple, and Smile that are Thai. So much impressive feeling you will get if you've seen." —ad for a Thailand promotional group.

So much impressive feeling, indeed. To mountain bike Thailand is to undergo any number of head changes. Thailand, after all, is the only country in Southeast Asia that's never been colonized. Its ancient mysteries have never been subjugated to Eurocentric pressures. Even today, Thailand delivers on the exotic promises made by the dilemmas of *The King and I,* the landscapes of *The Deer Hunter*, and the tastes of satay served at your local Thai restaurant. Bike in the northern part of the country, and every revolution of your pedal around the chainring will seem to spin your brain as well.

Cycling through one of the many hill tribe peasant villages north of Chiang Mai.

Consider:

Cultural Thailand: In the abrupt tropical mountains north of the city of Chiang Mai resides a culture so exotic it's been called the "Fourth World." This is the land of the hill tribes, a people who have preserved their way of life with little change over thousands of years. The tribes are mostly preliterate societies. Originating in various parts of China and Southeast Asia, the hill tribes are migrants who continue to migrate without regard for established national boundaries (hence, a Fourth World). They live in houses built on stilts and sometimes in houses with dirt floors. Most welcome adventurous, respectful visitors.

Natural Thailand: A quarter of Thailand is covered by monsoon forest or rain forest, and the country has an incredible array of fruit trees, bamboo, and tropical hardwoods. One northern province, Mae Hong Son, is made almost entirely of densely forested mountains: An amazing 80 percent of it sits on a slope of at least 45 degrees. Some peaks rise as high as 7,800 feet. There are more than 850 resident and migratory species of birds. Back roads will take you through wildlife reserves where tiger, elephant, and bear roam the jungle.

Spiritual Thailand: Buddhism is the dominant religion, and orange-robed monks and gold, marble, and stone Buddhas are common sights. Thai Buddhism emphasizes compassion, respect, and moderation—qualities that seem natural to express at the serene temples. The hill tribes, meanwhile, strive for harmony in relationships between individuals and the environment. Throughout Thailand, cyclists will see spirit houses—tiny temples on pedestals that shelter the forest ghosts displaced by human habitation.

Narcotic Thailand: Leaving China, the Mekong River slides between Myanmar and Laos, serving as the border, then touches Thailand. The misty area where the three countries meet is the Golden Triangle, where most of the world's opium is harvested and processed. The Thai government has succeeded in quelling drug-related violence in the area, making it safe for tourism. Still, opium has hardly gone away. Its presence, both in specific brainpans and in the general "lawless frontier" vibe, make the Golden Triangle an

---

AT A GLANCE

TRIP LENGTH 9 days
PHYSICAL CHALLENGE 1 2 ③ 4 5
MENTAL CHALLENGE 1 2 3 ④ 5
PRIME TIME October–February

PRICE RANGE (INDEPENDENT TRIP) $300
PRICE RANGE (OUTFITTED GROUP TRIP) $600–$800
STAGING CITY Chiang Mai, Thailand
HEADS UP The Golden Triangle doesn't smile on off-trail snooping

Top: Thai women at a floating market.
Above: Taking a break during a ride in the rain.

include hot and sour fish ragout, green and red curries, soups, and noodle dishes. Thais like to snack on healthy—or at least not overly filling—food all the time, so everywhere you ride, you'll encounter small, fragrant-smelling stands peddling hot delicacies.

Visitors to Thailand may not fully experience it on the small islands with great beaches or in the traffic- and pollution-choked megalopolis of Bangkok. But they will if they base a bike trip from Chiang Mai—an international city known for its universities, convenient public transportation, interesting nightlife, and warm weather.

Thailand's second-largest city and the gateway to the country's north, Chiang Mai was founded in 1296. You can still see the moat that encircled the original city. Bikes are the best way of seeing the old town, and of getting to the attractions outside the moat. Anthropologists probably consider the hill tribes the main attraction. Perhaps mountain bikers do, too. But they, at least, will appreciate the landscape: endless rolling scrub hills that evoke Appalachia—until one sees pockets of lush tropical vegetation, bamboo, and cloud forest. Woven into the humid greenery is an extensive maze of dirt road, doubletrack, and singletrack. Creeks and rivers split drainages littered with vines, mushrooms, and orchids.

A particularly detail-oriented rider said this about the Chiang Mai area's mtb opportunities: "Before you know it, you're off-road. A maze of track takes you through cattle pasture, fruit orchards (mango, litchi, jack fruit), a rubber plantation, eucalyptus groves, a linen field, a palm garden, soy fields, rice paddies, and a patchwork of small reservoirs feeding this land through the long dry months. You'll probably want to stop at the lake surrounded by bougainvillea and poinsettia to look at the carp, or perhaps pause at the palm garden for a short rest and your tour leader will offer oranges and peanut brittle."

Not that Northern Thailand is some magical

intoxicating and mesmerizing place to ride.

Gastronomic Thailand: Thai cuisine is pungent and spicy, seasoned with heaps of garlic and chilies and a characteristic mix of lime juice, lemon grass, and fresh coriander. Main dishes

Freshly planted rice paddies near a village north of Chiang Mai.

Shangri-La. Like much of Asia, it can be polluted with the exhaust of motorcycles or the smoke of slash-and-burn agriculture. The fact that it's never been colonized means it's accustomed to outsiders in its midst. It draws legions of travelers from all over the globe, and seems happy to embrace the West's excesses. The "Coca-Cola-nization" of Thailand may have seemed complete to the recent hill tribe visitors who encountered a witch doctor wearing a hooded Yale sweatshirt.

But the Thai have a phrase for such bothers: *Mai pen rai.* Translated as something like "never mind," it is said often. It basically echoes the Thai belief that the enjoyment of life should never be dampened by petty matters. Global homogeneity certainly merits worry and concern, but it shouldn't stop you from riding Thailand.

Go to the country's northern mountains. Perhaps one day, you'll wake before dawn to maximize your time in Thailand's cooler, less fre-

netic mornings. You'll navigate woods where falling teak leaves the size of dinner plates startle you with their noise. You'll ride a path of red dirt to high, forested saddle and watch as waves of mist breathe over the armies of dense green trees. You'll listen to the faint clanking of bells ringing from the valley, the sound of water buffalo trudging to their fields. At that sublime moment, perhaps you'll remember a small nugget of wisdom where biking and Thai-style Buddhism intersect. A joke, actually:

A Zen teacher saw three students returning from the market, riding their bicycles. When they arrived at the monastery and had dismounted, the teacher asked them, "Why are you riding your bicycles?"

The first student replied, "I love to watch the trees and fields pass by as I roll down the path!" The teacher commended the first student, "Your eyes are open, and you see the world."

Sometimes the only way to continue on singletrack is to pick the bike up and carry it.

The second student replied, "Riding my bicycle, I live in harmony with all sentient beings." The teacher was pleased, and said to the second student, "You are riding on the golden path of non-harming."

The third student replied, "I ride my bicycle to ride my bicycle." The teacher sat at his feet and said, "I am your student!"

WHAT TO EXPECT

Thailand shares borders with Malaysia, Myanmar (Burma), Laos, and Cambodia in Southeast Asia. From abroad, you'll likely fly into Bangkok (the steamy, lascivious capital) first. From there, you can get to Chiang Mai via plane, bus, or train. Thai International has a useful domestic flight network, but budget travelers tend to prefer Thailand's good bus and train transport. Buses are phenomenally (read hair-raisingly) fast, and they're also well serviced and air-conditioned. Trains are comfortable, frequent, punctual, moderately priced, and rather slow.

Although bicycles are popular transportation devices in Thai cities, recreational riding is still a somewhat esoteric pursuit. However, Northern Thailand has long catered to trekkers and other mountain explorers. You should bring the tools, tubes, and miscellaneous gear that will make you a self-sufficient rider, but you won't have to worry about finding inexpensive lodging or about not speaking the language.

Northern Thailand's hilly but not severe topography makes for ideal mtb terrain. Yet keep in mind that the roads were built for oxen or cars, and the trails were built for pedestrians. So the riding can involve stretches of road where trucks splatter you with mud, or trails where texture or tilt require you to carry the bike.

For climate considerations, the best overall time for visiting most of Thailand is between November and February: During these months it rains the least and is not too hot. The north is best from mid-November to early December or when it starts warming up again in February.

For general information, contact the U.S. office of the Tourism Authority of Thailand (312-819-3990; http://www.tat.or.th).

LODGING

One of the best guest houses in Chiang Mai is Gap's House (66-053-278140), a leafy compound with a nice bar and rooms that boast both air conditioning and hot showers.

In the Golden Triangle village of Sop Ruak,

Opposite: Traditional stone carving, Chiang Mai, Thailand.

A maze of empty dirt back roads is woven into the humid greenery.

check out Le Meridien Baan Boran (66-053-784086), a fine hotel that encourages exploration of the Mekong River valley by renting mountain bikes.

In Tha Ton, the Maekok River Lodge (66-053-459328; reservation@siam-hotel.com) runs mtb day trips (as well as river rafting and trekking tours) from its traditional teak building.

THE RIDES

The ride from Chiang Mai to Chiang Rai is an excellent Northern Thailand standby for mtb tourers. Normally taking four days, it skirts rural back roads and dirt trails while taking travelers to hill tribe meetings and cave explorations.

From the Chiang Mai area's Royal Phuping Palace, at about 4,000 feet above sea level, you can blast an exciting downhill. First, drop down to the Doi Pui Hmong hill tribe village. Once through the village, you're into forestry department singletrack. From that point on, you won't see another person or car or motorcycle for hours: What you will see is cloud forest canopy, wild palms, creeks you can drink water from and views of national park and the valleys lying hundreds of feet below.

The Chiang Dao Basin is ringed by high, craggy pinnacles including the Doi Luang—one of Thailand's highest. Impressive landscapes of limestone rocks and dense bamboo forest surround its network of trails and rough roads. Many hill tribes augment the valley's anthropological attractions.

A STENCH TO SAVOR

It's been said that the essence of Thailand is expressed in its fruits—exotic, sweet to the taste, and almost infinite in variety. But the local durian fruit is another matter entirely. A prickly skinned fruit with a thick shell, it's sometimes regarded as an offensive weapon in Thailand. It looks like a pineapple crossed with an armadillo. Yet inside is succulent, custard-like fruit with such intoxicating sweetness that sometimes a single durian sells for $200. But there's a catch: The durian's dreamy taste is accompanied by a nightmarish smell. Indeed, its stench—commonly likened to dog poop and overripe Limburger cheese—is so foul that Thai hotels and airplanes ban it from their confines. Is durian worth it? Well, as one wag put it, "Eating durian is like sitting on the toilet eating your favorite ice cream."

Mae Hang Son, the capital of the same-named province, is called the "City of Three Mists" due to the precipitation wafting from its deep valleys. The countryside around Mae Hang Son boasts a number of rides, including those to the Ban Pha Bong hot springs and Pha Sua waterfalls.

The Mekong Valley is significantly flatter than most of Northern Thailand. But its scenery is lush, and along its banks life continues much as it has for centuries. By day farmers grow rice, tamarinds and mangoes. At dawn and dusk they ply the river's surface with their dugout longboats searching for fish.

OUTFITTERS AND BIKE SHOPS

There are a number of bike rental operations along the eastern moat of Chiang Mai, but none stand out as a reliable place to service your beloved steed. If you need shop services, poke around the eastern moat and see what operations have decent tools and speak your language.

There are several outfitters in Chiang Mai. Perhaps the best for die-hard riders is Green Pedal Tours, a Thai-Italian outfit that rides dirt roads and singletrack through jungle, plateaus, and various mountain ranges (including those in the Golden Triangle). Green Pedal rents front-suspended bikes and can customize tours to be as long and challenging as you wish.

Other outfitters include Northern Trails Mountain-Biking Adventures, a dedicated mtb tour operator that offers a variety of fully supported excursions in the northern mountains. Torsak & Katie Murray Tiparos run a relatively gentle tour of the Mekong Valley.

GREEN PEDAL TOURS

Moon Muang Road
Chiang Mai, Thailand
http://thailandbicycles.hypermart.net/green.html
$45 per day
(no phone)

NORTHERN TRAILS MOUNTAIN-BIKING ADVENTURES

73/7 Charoen Prathet Road
Chiang Mai, Thailand
66-053-277-178
adventure@thailine.com
$70 per day

ONE WORLD BICYCLE EXPEDITIONS

Torsak & Katie Murray Tiparos
356 Chaikong Road
Chiang Khan, Loei 42110, Thailand
66-42-821-825
www.bikethailand.com
$1,435 for 10 days

RECOMMENDED READING

■ *THAILAND: THE ROUGH GUIDE* (1998. $19.95. The Rough Guides.) Specific mountain bike guidebooks are not yet available. But mountain bike tourism in the northern provinces is growing fast, and there may soon be such a book. In the meantime, the ideal map for biking the area is the "Chiang Mai and Thailand North Map" from Berndtson & Berndtson. It shows the crisscross of dirt tracks and minor roads on a 1:750,000 scale and includes the Golden Triangle.

■ *TRAVELER'S TALES: THAILAND,* edited by James O'Reilly and Larry Habegger (1993. $15.95. O'Reilly and Associates.) A whimsical collection of Thai adventures and commentary. The book's effect, if not its intention, is to celebrate Thailand's otherworldly experiences-whether the lurid details of its infamous sex trade, the atmosphere of its floating produce markets, or the sight of fish swimming around Bangkok's streets and cars during a flood.

PHOTO CREDITS

Jerry Alexander / Tony Stone Images: 209

Bob Allen: 14-15, 82-83, 89, 102 (bottom), 107, 140 (top), 145, 150, 152 (top), 174 (bottom), 176

Ian Austin / Aurora Productions: 29

José Azel / Aurora Productions: 52 (bottom), 92 (top), 142

Dirk Belling / Mercury Press: 118 (right), 158

Grilly Bernard / Tony Stone Images: 127

Nic Bothma: 162 (bottom)

Gary Braasch / Tony Stone Images: 133

Ernest Braun / Tony Stone Images: 183 (left), 200

Dugald Bremner: 16 (right), 42 (bottom), 48, 49, 56-57, 58, 62, 63

Skip Brown: 8, 152 (bottom), 153, 155, 174 (top), 177, 179, 181 (bottom)

John Callahan / Tony Stone Images: 194 (bottom)

Dan Campbell: 124

Robbie Caponetto: 159

Robert Caputo / Aurora Productions: 201

Carr Clifton / Minden Pictures: 136 (top), 148 (both), 151

Dennis Coello: 17 (right), 28 (top), 37, 44-45, 46, 47, 50, 64 (both), 67 (both), 68, 144, 180, 181 (top)

Cosmo Condina / Tony Stone Images: 119 (left), 170 (top)

Ron Dahlquist: 102 (top), 106, 108

Richard During / Tony Stone Images: 66

Siegfried Eigstler / Tony Stone Images: 164 (top)

Tim Flach / Tony Stone Images: 129

Henry Georgi: 17 (center), 60, 74

Ken Graham / Tony Stone Images: 25

Blaine Harrington: 26 (top), 28 (bottom), 33, 59, 120 (bottom), 128, 138 (top)

Bill Hatcher: 34 (top), 38, 40, 52 (top), 54, 61

Isaac Hernández / Mercury Press: 182 (right), 196, 198-199, 202

Neil Hourihane: 79

Johanna Huber / SIME: 17 (left), 80 (bottom), 84 (both)

Mark Jones / Minden Pictures: 146

John P. Kelly / Image Bank: 36

Jerry Kobalenko / Tony Stone Images: 197

Sterling Lorence: 72 (both), 75, 77, 78

David Madison: 118 (left), 132, 136 (bottom)

Flip McCririck: 26 (bottom), 30, 32, 91 (left), 110 (both), 112, 113, 115, 116, 117 (top)

Laurence Monneret / Tony Stone Images: 183 (right), 206 (top)

Tom Moran: 125, 166-167, 170 (bottom)

John Noltner / Aurora Productions: 207

David Paterson / Tony Stone Images: 194 (top)

Patrick Penkwitt / Mercury Press: 156 (bottom), 161, 172

David Reddick: 16 (left), 18 (both), 20, 21, 22-23, 24 (both)

Robert Rowan / Tony Stone Images: 130 (top)

Galen Rowell: 122-123,

David Sanger: 104, 105, 163, 192

Kevin Schafer: 143

Reinhard Schmid / SIME: 114

Mark Shapiro: 11, 119 (right), 164 (bottom), 168, 169, 173

Randy Sidman / Index Stock Imagery: 138 (bottom)

Giovanni Simeone / SIME: 2-3, 6, 9, 80 (top), 85, 86, 91 (right), 94, 117 (bottom), 156 (top)

Philip & Karen Smith / Tony Stone Images: 69

Scott Spiker: 10, 12, 42 (top), 55, 90 (both), 95, 96-97, 98, 100 (all), 101

Hugh Sitton / Tony Stone Images: 162 (top)

Jess Stock / Tony Stone Images: 140 (bottom)

Peter Straub: 204 (both), 206 (bottom), 208, 210

Ralph Talmont / Aurora Productions: 147

Aaron Teasdale: 182 (left), 184 (both), 186, 187, 188, 190, 191

Darryl Torckler / Tony Stone Images: 120 (top)

Penny Tweedie / Tony Stone Images: 126

Beth Wald / Aurora Productions: 71

John Warden / Tony Stone Images: 130 (bottom)

Dennis Waugh / Tony Stone Images: 92 (bottom)

David B. Wilkins: 34 (bottom), 41

Konrad Wothe / Minden Pictures: 141

George Wuerthner: 135

INDEX